MW00425363

Inclusion Nudges Guidebook:

Practical Techniques for Changing Behaviour, Culture & Systems to Mitigate Unconscious Bias and Create Inclusive Organisations

Tinna C. Nielsen - Founder

Move the Elephant for Inclusiveness
Info@movetheelephant.org
www.movetheelephant.org
www.inclusion-nudges.org

Lisa Kepinski - Founder

Inclusion Institute
lisa.kepinski@inclusion-institute.com
www.inclusion-institute.com
www.inclusion-nudges.org

Edition: 2, January 2016 © T. Nielsen & L. Kepinski, 2016
www.inclusion-nudges.org

Table of Contents

Section 5: EXAMPLES OF "FRAMING" INCLUSION NUDGES 148

INCLUSION NUDGES
Practical Techniques for Changing Behaviour, Culture and Systems to Mitigate
Unconscious Bias and Create Inclusive Organisations

Section 1: INTRODUCTION

HOW TWO PERSONAL JOURNEYS LED TO A GLOBAL MOVEMENT OF SHARING

This Guidebook contains practical techniques to promote behaviour, culture and system change to mitigate unconscious bias and create inclusive organisations. The examples come from the authors and other practitioners in the field of inclusion and diversity. The authors call these practical techniques Inclusion Nudges.

The Guidebook is the result of a mutual friend[1] connecting us during the spring of 2013. Tinna C. Nielsen and Lisa Kepinski have both worked as internal Inclusion & Diversity (I&D)[2] experts and cultural change agents in several organisations over many years (our biographies are at the end of this Guidebook). Sharing our work challenges, failures, and successes led us to merge our similar approaches to behaviour, culture and system change. In doing so, we developed a framework for what we have named Inclusion Nudges. We are now sharing this worldwide.

Tinna, an anthropologist and behavioural economist, has specialised in organisational cultural, behavioural change, and I&D for more than 14 years. As Global Head of Inclusion, Diversity & Collaboration at Arla Foods, where she worked (2010-15), she focused on creating a unique, more sustainable path to inclusion by applying neuroscience, anthropology, psychology and nudging techniques. Lisa has been a senior global leader in I&D for more than 20 years in multinational organisations (Hewlett-Packard, Microsoft, & AXA) and has a background in social psychology and socio-linguistics. Throughout her career, she has used many techniques to promote inclusive behaviour change. We both follow the latest research and trends in various fields related to our work; at the same time, we're very pragmatic about sorting through all the "stuff" out there and seeing how it can practically apply to the workplace. No single researcher or book primarily influenced us as we developed the concept of Inclusion Nudges. We've drawn heavily from our experience as internal I&D leaders and have synthesized a wide range of research on human motivation, decision-making, thinking and behavioural change to create the techniques of Inclusion Nudges. We have applied these ourselves, and shared with others about these and how to use them, as we work to bring about change in simple yet effective ways inside organisations.

In our work, we use a very broad definition of inclusion: it means removing all excluding barriers and promoting mindsets, behaviour, processes and practices that embrace differences. By leveraging diverse perspectives, skills and backgrounds, it's possible to realize the full potential of each individual, team, and organisation. Our mission is to promote more sustainable organisational success worldwide through high engagement, inclusive leadership, equality, social responsibility, and innovative collaboration.

In our own collaboration, we have drawn upon our experiences with the challenges of creating inclusive and diverse organisations. We assume that most readers who are involved with driving culture change have had the experience of moving three steps forward and then one step back, or felt the frustration of seeing the organisation move forward only to find out later that many people have reverted to default behaviour. We also assume that most readers have been concerned about how to get thousands of people to move in the same direction – in our case, towards a more inclusive culture – while at the same time allowing them to get there in as many different ways as there are people in the organisation. Like us, some of you might have found that the best I&D programs, policies, initiatives, and training sessions didn't pay off as fast or as much in behavioural and cultural changes as anticipated. Based on these personal experiences, we've experimented over the years with techniques from the science of behavioural economics, applying insights from psychology, neuroscience, and microeconomic theory to make a crucial difference.

Behavioural economics targets the false assumption that almost all people, nearly all of the time, make choices and act in ways that are in their own best interest or the best interest of the organisations where they work. Approaches based on behavioural economics influence people to act in a predictable way and direction, steer people to make better choices, and "push" the unconscious system of the brain in a non-intrusive way to change behaviour, without taking away their freedom to choose.

We did not design the framework of Inclusion Nudges with the intent of writing a "how-to" book or creating a new buzzword. We were motivated by our passion for I&D work, our frustration with the typical approaches, and the personal challenges of being a change agent within organisations. Inclusion Nudges spring from a need to find new ways to help people change behaviour without making it hard and without allowing their unconscious mind to work against their professed intentions to be truly inclusive. We wrote this Guidebook due to a request from peers on how to apply these techniques.

These techniques are not *the* solution to developing true inclusive and diverse organisations. We use them in our work as a supplement to, not a substitute for, I&D programmes, initiatives and trainings such as cultural competency training, reverse mentoring, sponsorship, unconscious bias awareness, flexible/agile working, and more. We have coined the term Inclusion Nudges and developed a framework to apply this systematically in our own work and now to share with others. We operate with three types of Inclusion Nudges that target motivation, ability/simplicity, and perception. We will introduce these with examples from our own experience and from many contributors. We will also introduce how you can design Inclusion Nudges in your own organisation.

After six months of working together virtually, Tinna and Lisa met in person for the first time in a park in Mannheim, Germany, in 2013. The very next day, we kick-started what we call *a global movement of sharing for inclusiveness*. This Guidebook is a major step in the global movement. When submitting an example for the Guidebook the contributor receives all the published examples in return free of charge. By sharing the techniques and examples of powerful Inclusion Nudges with change agents in organisations worldwide, we believe we can inspire others and together create a profound shift in the current approach to organisational development and Inclusion & Diversity in the 21st Century.

WHY INCLUSION NUDGES?

The global world is changing at a speed never experienced before due to technological development, knowledge production, and changes in the demographic make-up of the workforce. As cognitive, cultural, and demographic diversity continues to grow, individuals and organisations must be able to interact and make decisions in an increasingly complex environment. To remain agile and innovative, we need to leverage the diversity of perspectives and knowledge available to us in our organisations, teams, schools, communities, and societies. Only then can we put into play our full potential and resources. This requires organisations as well as individuals to seek out diversity, promote more inclusion, and mitigate all unconscious biases and excluding mechanisms in processes, practices, and cultures. *This is not news*. Decades of research and case studies have proven I&D's importance to business. Organisations have invested much effort and resources in I&D programs, each with its own business case, broad commitment to non-discrimination and equity, and diversity data reports. So why, with all these good intentions, do we not see more progress and behavioural change?

The underlying issue is that the human brain has not learned to deal with this new environment. Though we like to believe we are rational thinkers, 80 to 90% of the time we're actually relying on the automatic, subconscious system of the brain to make decisions. This automatic system evolved to ensure our survival; however, the world is vastly more complex today. The brain has to manage more than 11 million bits of information at any given moment, and shortcuts have evolved to accomplish this without using a lot of energy. In most cases it works, but in many other cases, errors in judgment are made, which are *not* registered in the conscious mind. Unconscious biased thinking is universal; more than 150 common biases have been identified to date. These may be in direct conflict with our intention to give people equal opportunities and make rational decisions rooted in inclusion.

Many organisations today use unconscious bias training to increase understanding and awareness of these deeply embedded, implicit associations. This often results in insightful discussions that engage a wide range of leaders and employees because we *all* have biases (regardless of gender, nationality, sexual orientation, age, level in the organisation, etc.). However, more and more I&D practitioners note that awareness is insufficient to mitigate the impact of unconscious associations and promote sustainable inclusive behaviours. The critical junction point after training is where many organisations get stuck. The issue of how to move beyond awareness of unconscious bias to inclusive behaviours is currently a topic of widespread debate among I&D practitioners, many of whom are searching for a practical process that will produce lasting results.

We were inspired to launch this project to fulfil the need for practical applications of unconscious bias awareness. We were also motivated by the need for enablers to create awareness of unconscious bias that would lead to behavioural change. Key is to have impact of these enablers outside of training sessions, and integrated in stakeholder management, process design, leadership interactions, facilitation, communication, etc. Often leaders and colleagues ask the I&D practitioner, "*What next?*" after a training session. Our reaction was "*Let's share what has worked for us and hear from others about what has worked for them.*" We believe that awareness of how our unconscious mind works and the impact of unconscious bias in organisational situations is a crucial first step towards greater equality and better business performance. But a rational understanding and awareness is not enough. It is also a challenge to create this awareness outside of training/learning activities, thus a more innovative approach is required. The purpose of Inclusion Nudges is to help the brain change behaviour by targeting motivation, emotions, behavioural drivers, decision-making, and unconscious perceptions. We have seen first-hand how this can strengthen leadership, collaboration, and performance as a result of more inclusiveness.

In this Guidebook, we introduce you to three types of Inclusion Nudges that have worked for us and for other practitioners. Using the employee life cycle and organisational culture as our framework, we have focused on the micro-decision points: the moments when we have an opportunity to outsmart our brain and prod it towards decisions more aligned with our stated intentions of inclusiveness. We've found that with a micro-intervention, such as an Inclusion Nudge, at these crucial points, we can generate macro-changes in bias mitigation and create more inclusive cultures.

Our hope is that this Guidebook will inspire you to practice designing and implementing Inclusion Nudges within your organisations. We sincerely thank everyone who submitted examples for this first edition, and we look forward to receiving more examples to share in future editions. Please visit the book's website and become a part of the Inclusion Nudges Global Community (www.inclusion-nudges.org) to continue your interactive experience with Inclusion Nudges and to be a part of the dialogue in this global sharing initiative for inclusive organisations.

Tinna C. Nielsen and Lisa Kepinski

ACKNOWLEDGEMENTS

This book would not have been possible without the participation of our many colleagues around the world. We received contributions from Japan, Australia, China, India, South Africa, Spain, Austria, France, Belgium, the Netherlands, Germany, Denmark, the UK, Switzerland, Liechtenstein, the U.S., Canada, Mexico, Brazil, and more. We deeply thank you for your participation in this project.

We also thank the organizations that have given us a platform to share the concept of Inclusion Nudges over the past year, some of these are the United Nation's WEP, Lynda Gratton's Hot Spots Movement, The Conference Board (both in Europe and the US), WIN, ICON, The German Diversity Charter, The City of Copenhagen's Diversity Network, and many more. Also we have appreciated the companies that have brought us into their teams to share about Inclusion Nudges, sometimes through presentations and other times through full-day Inclusion Nudges Learning Labs. We have valued the support and feedback that has been shared with us throughout this period. This continued to inspire us to keep going as we saw how our colleagues from around the world positively and enthusiastically embraced the concept and we saw what a difference Inclusion Nudges makes in not only our own work but in these companies as well.

In addition, our thanks go to Tinna's employer during this period, Arla Foods, for its generous support of her work outside the company. We are grateful to Julie O'Mara for sharing her experience with the publication of *Global Diversity & Inclusion Benchmarks*, an outstanding document drawing on the work of more than 80 experts, which is available free of charge[3]. Thanks to Camila Kepinski who allowed us to use her illustrations in this book and in our Inclusion Nudges presentations. (For permission to reprint these, please contact Lisa Kepinski.) Thank you to Christina & Henry Muller for their editing of the manuscript. Any errors are the authors' own, especially given our continuing revisions after their editing process. Much appreciation goes to Anne-Mette Hansen for her creative help with designing the Guidebook's cover, logos, and graphic scheme for the Inclusion Nudges website. Equally, much appreciation goes to Tanja Arnholtz Nielsen for her expertise on setting up the Inclusion Nudges website, giving us the platform to have the Inclusion Nudges Global Community. Our gratitude also goes to Eric Dziedzic for originally introducing Lisa and Tinna.

And, a very important thank you to our families for their support during our *many* long hours on this project over the past year and half. It has been a period of much change for us, and keeping on with the project was often at the expense of time from our families, and also often going late, late into the night on top of full days. Throughout, we have valued their loving support of us, and their confidence and belief in what we sought to accomplish.

In this first edition, we've listed below the names of all colleagues who submitted a contribution, whether it was used or not (in some cases, the submissions were great examples of I&D practices and programmes rather than Inclusion Nudges). The contributors' organisations are not listed on this page. Some contributors chose to list their affiliation with their example. Please note that people may no longer be with the same company at publication time and that the examples given may have been used at a previous employer. Should you wish to contact contributors, kindly use LinkedIn and/or reach out to Lisa & Tinna.

CONTRIBUTORS

1. Abigail Hiza
2. Alberto Platz
3. Alexa Mbowa
4. Alison Maitland
5. Anita Cassagne
6. Anita Curle
7. Ann Dunkin
8. Axel Jenztsch
9. Annette Stausholm
10. Barbara Hopland
11. Ben Capell
12. Carol Putnam
13. Charlotte Sweeney
14. Cindy Gallop
15. Debbie Esptein
16. Elaine Yarbrough
17. Eric Dziedzic
18. Flavia Micilotta
19. Flora Marriott
20. Gina Badenoch
21. Gudrun Sander
22. Howard Ross
23. Iris Bohnet
24. Janina Norton
25. Jo Ann Morris
26. Jolanda Verbeek
27. Josefine van Zanten
28. Julie O'Mara
29. Juliet Bourke
30. Karin Middelburg van Goinga
31. Karsten Jonsen
32. Katrien Van Eetvelde
33. Kevin Bradley
34. Leslie Traub
35. Lisa Kepinski
36. Louise Harringe
37. Lut Nelissen
38. Manon de Jongh
39. Martin Swain
40. Nia Joynson-Romanzina
41. Renee Anderson
42. Richard Spada
43. Sarah Boddey
44. Sarah Margles
45. Sergio Franca Leao
46. Sharon Kyle
47. Stephen Frost
48. Sue Johnson
49. Suzanne Price
50. Susanne Justesen
51. Thais Compoint
52. Tinna C. Nielsen
53. Ulla Dalgaard
54. Ursula A. Wynhoven
55. Verna Myers
56. Veronika Hucke
57. Virginia Argarate
58. Yves Veulliet

... and more contributors (some wished to remain anonymous)

HOW TO USE THIS GUIDEBOOK

Inspiration for Designing Your Own Inclusion Nudges

As we've experienced in our own practice, there is no "one size fits all" in I&D work. Each solution needs to be carefully attuned to its organisational context. This is also true with Inclusion Nudges. The examples here are intended as inspiration, not a step-by-step guide; you may not get the same result – or even any result – in your organisation if you simply apply the same Inclusion Nudge as the person who contributed it. Only some Inclusion Nudges will be applicable in most organisations. Instead, look at these examples as a starting point for your own. You can become adept at designing Inclusion Nudges only by experimenting and practising in your own real-life settings. We hope this Guidebook will spark further curiosity and experimentation. Designing Inclusion Nudges is something everyone can learn and that all internal agents of change should master. You can get assistance by contacting the authors directly and by visiting the Inclusion Nudge website (**www.inclusion-nudges.org**).

To keep this Guidebook reader-friendly, we opted not to include multiple citations and endnotes. The studies and practices we refer to are well documented; you'll also find a comprehensive reference section at the end that lists books, journal articles, websites, and videos. Also we have re-written most of the submissions to align to the Guidebook format and added our own 'AUTHORS' COMMENTS' as a tutorial contribution.

Permission Process

Though we have coined the term Inclusion Nudge and developed the framework of the three types of Inclusion Nudges, we have not copyrighted these concepts because we believe in sharing and professional trust. In support of this approach, we have applied the Creative Commons Attribution-Non-Commercial-Share Alike 4.0 International license[4] to this work, the Guidebook, and the website's content. We ask that the Guidebook be limited to the reader's own personal use and that it not be distributed or used by consultancies to develop any derivative (commercial) products without our written permission. If you wish to excerpt material, please attribute the Guidebook, its authors, and the contributing source of the Inclusion Nudge, if any. We reserve the right to change the permission process if these requests are not honoured. Our hope and expectation is that the spirit of professional courtesy, trust, and respect will prevail.

KEEPING THE GLOBAL MOVEMENT GOING

There will be future editions of this Guidebook, so we encourage readers to submit their examples of Inclusion Nudges. We would also be grateful if contributors to this edition would share any updates about their example. Please contact us if you have any questions.

Lisa Kepinski: **lisa.kepinski@inclusion-institute.com**

Tinna Nielsen: **tinna@movetheelephant.org**

We hope you will visit **www.inclusion-nudges.org** to share your examples, learn more about behavioural insights, Inclusion Nudges, and neuroscience, and to get inspiration from free resources. On Twitter, follow Tinna on **#tinnaCnielsen** and Lisa on **#InclusionInst**.

Section 2: INCLUSION NUDGES

WHY INCLUSION & DIVERSITY WORK CAN GET STUCK

Inclusion in the workplace is focused on fostering the structure, culture, and mindset that creates a feeling in employees that they "fit" – in other words that they are valued and able to contribute to their fullest. Inclusion is also about ensuring that diversity of knowledge, perspectives, and information is sought and applied in the way we solve tasks and make decisions. Diversity is about the people themselves – their demographic differences, backgrounds, multiple identities, and unique experiences and perspectives. Diversity is also about patterns of behaviour such as how we staff our teams, how and with whom we network, how and to whom we give feedback, and for whom we design and develop a market. Often patterns of behaviour are dominated by homogeneity, thus limiting access to the diversity and potential available in a workforce, workplace, and market. When you combine a highly inclusive culture with a diverse workforce, the results can have an impact on organisational success in terms of better decision-making, teamwork and collaboration, financial return, customer/market perspectives, innovation, and talent engagement.

Some organisations may start by targeting diverse talent. Others may begin with inclusion by targeting cultural transformation. Many organisations do both. The motivations may include better business performance, human rights, compliance, legal requirements, values, a moral imperative ("the right thing to do"), shareholder pressure, keeping up with peer companies, and global benchmarking. Regardless of the starting point and the motivation, I&D initiatives lay the groundwork for the attraction, development, promotion, and retention of talent – and for better performance. Though the research is not conclusive, numerous findings from academia, think tanks, and internal organisational research indicate that I&D is a business imperative.

Yet so often we have seen huge effort, passion, and commitment put into launching I&D projects which have limited lasting impact. For example, *decades* of women's mentoring programmes have been rolled out around the world, and indeed still are being conducted in organisations today. However, the number of women at senior executive levels is not even close to the number of women who have been through these programs nor does it mirror the percentage of women in the organisation's workforce. It is often said that women are "over-mentored". Even so, in organisations that make gender inclusion a priority, someone well-meaning will fairly quickly say "we must put in a women's mentoring program." Considerable energy and resources will be dedicated to women's mentoring with the belief that it will be the magic solution for rectifying the decreasing numbers of women at senior levels.

There is a gap between many I&D initiatives and the actual achievement of desired goals. Overall, we see several reasons for this limited progress, including:

- **COMPLIANCE Approach:** Metrics (internal and/or external) drive the work, often with the entire focus on meeting these targets. The overall purpose and intended outcomes are not understood. A punitive culture evolves around I&D work, which increases negative backlash and limits commitment to change. While we firmly believe metrics play an important role in I&D work, they should be *indicators* of progress, not the beginning and end points.

- **CHARISMATIC PERSONALITY Approach:** I&D initiatives are tied to the championship of individual leaders and I&D specialists; when the leader moves on or the business undergoes a change, the I&D program struggles, as it was not tied to a business strategy.

- **FIX THE DIFFERENCE Approach:** Under the banner of "inclusion", the initiatives focus nearly entirely on helping the "minority"[5] rather than also engaging the majority and changing the implicit norms in the organisation. Without including the majority, progress will remain a "minority" issue and the organisational culture will not be addressed.

- **YOU CAN'T TOUCH THIS Approach:** Changing the organisational culture is off-limits, so there is no focus on changing the implicit norms of the organisational culture or the ways of working. The same-old stays the same-old. Every individual continues to perform, behave, communicate, and look in a specific (unwritten and unsaid) way. The privileged remain privileged. Innovation suffers. Status quo stagnation and groupthink can occur.

- **FINGER POINTING & FINGER WAGGING Approach**: Unproductive side effects emerge from an unspoken culture of "blame and shame". This breaks down any hope for sustainable inclusive partnerships across differences and contributes to an 'us-and-them' culture. I&D

cannot be discussed due to politically correct communication styles that shut down open, honest dialogue.

- **BUSY BEES Approach:** Numerous programs are done on the surface, without the needed core organisational development (OD) work that addresses systemic issues in a healthy, sustainable manner. Short-term results are sought and spotlighted. This results in exhaustion, not to mention wasted resources and limited long-term change.

You might experience other reasons for limited progress on I&D efforts.

Without a doubt, both Inclusion and Diversity must be addressed in any organisational culture-change initiative. They must be an integrated part of the organisation's DNA. But rather than calling out one approach as better than another, we suggest a starting point of facilitating behavioural, cultural, and systemic changes simultaneously by using behavioural economics techniques. These apply to every organisation regardless of I&D approach, motivation, starting point, and history.

TARGETING THE WHOLE BRAIN

To promote behavioural change and improve decision making, we must work with the subconscious. As psychologist Jonathan Haidt illustrates in *The Happiness Hypothesis* and the Heath brothers discuss in *Switch*[6], it's as difficult to change the unconscious mind as it is to move an unmotivated six-ton heavy elephant. Willpower and rational intentions are far from enough. By appealing to the unconscious part of the brain, we can more successfully act on the intentions we state through the rational part of our brain. For example, simply asserting, even with passion and enthusiasm, "*I want to be more inclusive in my approach to people who are different*" will rarely generate a sustainable change in behaviour. Or hearing leaders say, "*I believe in diversity*" does not always produce the behavioural changes needed to leverage diversity for better performance, engagement, or equal opportunity. So what can we do when the belief in I&D seems to be in place?

The practice of Inclusion and Diversity is often centred only on the reflective part of the brain – invoking, for example, the business case, demographic data, or the diversity of target markets. These approaches can keep the work solely on the rational level and can be an unintended block to solid commitments for change and progress. It is easier to resist change when it is positioned in a dry, numbers-only manner. People can keep asking for more data, dispute the evidence, or miss the stories behind the data. In trying to gain leaders' engagement and commitment to change, it may seem more "business like" to use a data-dominated approach. But by staying exclusively at this level, we haven't engaged the equally important subconscious. In order to achieve commitment to change, we need to appeal to the whole brain, using specifically designed approaches.

THE POWER OF THE SUBCONSCIOUS MIND

Generally, our thinking is described as occurring through two interdependent systems. In his book, *Thinking, Fast and Slow*, Daniel Kahneman describes "System 1" as fast, automatic, associative, emotional, irrational, and subconscious, which is centred in what is called our evolutionary "reptilian" or primitive brain. He describes "System 2" as the slow, controlled, reflective, rational, self-aware/conscious aspect of cognitive processing, centred in the evolutionary "newer" part of our brain, the neocortex. As much as we'd like to believe that we are logical, rational decision makers, we actually are not. Researchers have estimated that as much as 90% of our thought processes occur automatically; thus our behaviour is dominated by our subconscious (System 1). The most powerful drivers in this part of the brain are like/dislike, safe/unsafe, approach/withdraw and short cuts to save energy. This plays out through conformity, homogeneity, us-and-them categories, biases, and selective attention for good and bad. The downside of these very natural and useful processes can be the exclusion of individuals, groups of people, information, and knowledge – resulting in lost opportunities, regardless of good intentions to embrace diversity and be truly inclusive.

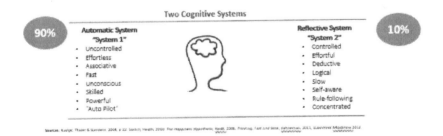

When making decisions we often use these mental shortcuts (heuristics), which are hard-wired in our brains by the evolutionary process. Sometimes these help, but sometimes not and they lead to errors. For example, deciding whom to call upon in a team meeting may be based on quick, unconscious perceptions of whom we like/dislike and can come at the cost of ignoring people who may have valuable contributions. Likewise, unconscious motivation factors and the chemical make-up of our brain also influence our thought processes and our ability to change. Paul J. Zak of Claremont Graduate University found that people are more likely to make a change when they are emotionally connected to a cause. Storytelling is a device that, when used with skill, can lead to higher releases of oxytocin, which is produced when we are trusted or shown a kindness – and it motivates cooperation with others. These are key to inclusive behaviours. So, when looking at ways to "...motivate, persuade, or be remembered, start with a story [*not a data report or long PowerPoint presentation!*].... It will capture people's hearts – by first attracting their brains."[7]

Extensive research on the unconscious, including Kahneman's, illustrates its impact on our beliefs, decisions, and behaviour. This comes into play when we evaluate employees and colleagues, select and promote candidates, network and process information. Also when we manage, deal with consumers, innovate, design, and communicate – basically everything we do as family members, citizens, and professionals. Yet we are not aware of it happening nor, for that matter, in control of it. Research findings illustrate, for example, how height has an impact on who is selected to top leadership positions. Sixty percent of male CEOs in the U.S. are more than 1.85m tall, compared to 14% of the general population. The tendency to select a taller candidate is strongly influenced by implicit associations between height and authority, visibility and strong presence[8] (similar studies have been done in Sweden and other countries, and also studies looking at heads of state and military leaders all with similar results of height and authority within measurements associated with the country's population). Other studies find that the same behaviour is evaluated differently depending on gender. When people are shown pictures of distressed baby girls and asked what feeling they are expressing, the majority will say anxiety; if the same infants are positioned as boys, they are perceived as angry[9]. A Stanford University professor[10] conducted the same experiment using the Harvard case study on successful Silicon Valley entrepreneur Heidi Roizen. He created a version of Heidi called Howard and asked MBA students to rate the two candidates. They found them equally competent, but Heidi was perceived too assertive, aggressive and selfish, and they would not seek her out for collaboration and not hire her.

Researchers have also found that accent plays a key role in who is included. Our brain resonates better with information if the speaker has the same accent as ours. Unconsciously, we find them more credible[11]. In *Reinventing Diversity*, Howard Ross provides a comprehensive collection of these crucial findings.

Even so, most of us genuinely believe we are independent individuals who will speak up even if others in a group think differently. We also believe that if we encourage people to share their views and beliefs candidly they will do so. But psychologist Salomon Asch proved with experiments on conformity in the 1950s that this is not the case. In a group, more than one third of people will conform to the views of the majority. The experiments also showed that simple interventions such as writing the answer instead of telling it to the group, or making allies within the group, reduced conformity by two thirds. Such interventions fit the framework of Inclusion Nudges because they help the brain make a better choice by creating more psychological safety. We are not as rational and objective as we would like to think.

Since the automatic and emotional-oriented system is in charge of our behaviour, it is crucial to target this part of the brain in order to leverage the potential of diversity and develop more inclusive organisations. We provide examples in this Guidebook that illustrate what kind of brain fallacies we are up against and how to challenge them.

With Inclusion Nudges, we have developed an approach that targets the advantages and shortcomings of our unconscious mind and decision-making processes in order to obtain the desired and needed changes. Techniques from behavioural economics can impact inclusiveness because they focus on how the human mind works and how to "outsmart" the unconscious mind.

BEHAVIOURAL ECONOMICS AND NUDGING TECHNIQUES

Thaler and Sunstein define a nudge as "... *any aspect of the choice architecture* [behavioural and decision-making context] *that alters people's behaviour in a predictable way without forbidding any options or significantly changing their economic incentives*".[12] A behavioural nudge is a relatively soft and non-intrusive mental push that will help the brain make better decisions. Furthermore Thaler and Sunstein describe a "good nudge" as a behavioural intervention (transparent and non-transparent) carried out to influence the choice and behaviour of other people in accordance with their own interests or good intentions. Nudging is a technique that helps people change behaviour without convincing them with rational arguments, setting up incitements, threatening or punishing them. A nudge is like choice architecture, where the environment, the system default, or the anchor of the thought process has been designed to help your unconscious mind automatically make a directed choice. It is a relatively passive change in behaviour: the person does not think actively about the change nor does he or she need to engage willpower to alter behaviour. Everyday life is full of such nudges; the following are four nudge examples and we briefly discuss how we have applied each concept to create the three types of "Inclusion Nudges".

"Directional" Nudge

Urinals have a flaw: some waste unintentionally ends up on the floor. To help reduce the mess, a sticker with the image of a fly is placed inside the bowl. The fly nudges men to aim better, ensuring cleaner facilities. Initiated at Amsterdam's Schiphol Airport, this approach has been replicated worldwide. Studies show a reduction in spillage of as much as 85%.[13]

We have applied this "Directional" Nudge to our work on Inclusion Nudges by focusing on steering behaviour in a predictable direction by making the destination clear without appealing to the rational part of the brain.

"Frame" Nudge

Most people want to be healthy, and that often means losing weight. Often people expend a lot of willpower – part of the brain's reflective system – to battle the automatic system in the brain that wants those cookies or that second portion. Rather than appeal to the rational brain by discussing portion control, calories or healthy food choices, a powerful nudge is to reduce plate size. With a smaller plate size, the unconscious system perceives the plate as full and thus feels full. In the photo, each plate contains the same amount. [14]

We have applied this "Frame" Nudge by focusing on changing the frame to create another perception of diversity, thus promoting the desired behaviour of more inclusion.

"Implicit Association" Nudge

In the early 1970s, Alexander Schauss conducted researched on the "calming effect" of the colour pink. Since then, the colour has been used successfully to reduce violence in prisons for men in the U.S., Switzerland, Australia and other countries. At the same time, another implicit association was triggered. The male inmates in a Texas prison wore pink clothing and the cells were pink, as were the sheets and towels. The result was not only less violence but also a 68% reduction in returning inmates. In Illinois, buses painted pink had much less graffiti than other buses. One explanation is that the colour pink signals a feminine domain; regardless of social background, the cultural norm is that "you don't hit girls; you protect girls" – not to mention that as a man you tend to avoid the colour.[15] [16]

We apply this "Implicit Association" Nudge by focusing on priming the brain to trigger a specific link that fosters inclusive behaviour and decision-making.

"Opt In/Opt Out" Nudge

When people are asked if they support organ donation, a sizeable majority says yes; one survey showed 97% in favour[17]. Yet when asked to register as an organ donor, only 43% did so. By changing the default, the complexity of a choice can be reduced – in this case by automatically registering all citizens as organ donors and asking them to opt out if they do not want to be registered.

We have applied this default rule and "Opt In/Opt Out" Nudge by focusing on designing systems and processes that reverse the default and challenge the organisational norms for performance, career, and skills.

Our work defining and designing Inclusion Nudges is the first instance we have come across of applying behavioural economics systematically to the area of Inclusion & Diversity (although some work has started recently on "Gender Nudges"[18]). In our interactions with key organisations, practitioners and researchers in the fields of behavioural economics, I&D, business management, HR and organisational development (OD)[19], we have received feedback calling this "ground-breaking" and "game-changing" work that the field of I&D especially needs.

Our focus is a broad view of inclusion, across all cognitive and demographic differences. For this Guidebook, we have chosen the workplace as the framework for Inclusion Nudges. This framework differs from the traditional types of nudges, both by embracing "passive" nudges like those described above and by applying others that are designed to be more "active".

The essential similarities between nudges and Inclusion Nudges are:

- Not using rational arguments alone to convince people
- Minimizing the negative impact of the shortcuts and biases of the unconscious mind
- Not relying on awareness, rationality, willpower and reflection as drivers for change
- Not using incitements, threats or punishment
- Respecting freedom of choice

But how does this promote more inclusiveness, and thus better decisions in organisations?

INCLUSION NUDGES

An Inclusion Nudge is a relatively soft and non-intrusive mental push (passive and active) that will mitigate unconscious associations, thus help the brain make more objective decisions, and promote more inclusive behaviours - that will stick.

We each felt that we needed a new tactic in our work. Over the years both of us have combined knowledge with techniques from psychology, behavioural economics, neuroscience, anthropology and other disciplines. Based on our personal experiences, we have joined forces to develop this framework. (For further research, please see the list of references at the end of this Guidebook.)

We have identified three types of Inclusion Nudges that address challenges in the employee life cycle and organisational culture. They target both the brain's reflective "System 2" and its automatic "System 1", unlike the passive behavioural nudges referred to in the previous section that target only the automatic system. We've experienced in practice what the RSA Social Brain project Steer[20] concludes: that only by taking a "holistic reflexive approach" to brain science can we improve how we navigate our automatic, controlled, and environmental impulses.

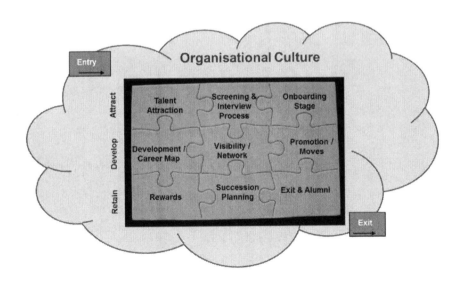

1. "FEEL THE NEED" Inclusion Nudge

These motivate people to change behaviour by making the brain's unconscious system *feel the need for change* rather than having only a rational understanding of the need for change. Often taking the form of eye-openers or "aha-moments", they are designed to show or illustrate rather than tell the brain how biased it is and warn of the consequences of the status quo. These Inclusion Nudges target emotions, both positive and negative – such as surprise, astonishment, disgust, empathy, and excitement. They take good intentions to the next level, producing buy-in for change, action with increased reflection and a new language to challenge the status quo. "FEEL THE NEED" Inclusion Nudges are also useful in bringing about compliance and accountability without linking I&D to rewards; instead, they create a follow-the-herd reaction, showing the inclusive behaviour of the majority.   Another positive side effect is to keep the I&D facilitator from becoming the target of negative emotions. Instead, the focus is oriented toward the outcome of the Inclusion Nudge when designed as an interactive intervention.

2. "PROCESS" Inclusion Nudge

This type of Inclusion Nudge is intended to help people *make better decisions* (more objective, less biased, more inclusive) by altering the system and elements in organisational processes, such as candidate screening, promotions, performance reviews, successor planning, team collaboration and decision-making. The main purpose is to make it easy to be inclusive – ability and simplicity is key. They steer the brain's unconscious system toward inclusiveness by changing the system default (such as *opt out* instead of *opt in*), altering the design of an organisational process or changing the data we see in a choice process. This type of Inclusion Nudge does not rely on rational understanding, willpower, or motivation. It is designed simply to mitigate the negative impact of unconscious bias and create a more inclusive thought process. "PROCESS" Inclusion Nudges can also be used in teamwork and facilitation of meetings to leverage diversity of thought and avoid conformity, while reducing the negative effects of group dynamics. They are also useful in creating compliance with training and capability requirements without using rewards as incentives.

3. "FRAMING" Inclusion Nudge

This type of Inclusion Nudge is intended to help people (the brain) perceive issues related to inclusion, diversity, equality in a resource discourse, and to prime specific associations and thus inclusive behaviours by altering the frame

© T. Nielsen & L. Kepinski, 2016
www.inclusion-nudges.org

or change the anchor of the thought process. Terms like diversity, inclusion, gender, and equality trigger some sensitivity for most people because they are associated with some kind of change, and the unconscious mind does not like the uncertainty that change brings. To avoid these automatic emotional reactions, we should aim to alter the connotations of such terms by designing Inclusion Nudges that prime positive – or at least neutral – associations. An effective approach is to alter certain factors, such as the order in which data is presented, the formulation of questions, the reporting of numbers and the setting of targets. For example, the focus can be shifted from *minority* to *majority* or from *increasing diversity* to *reducing homogeneity*.

The three types of Inclusion Nudges can be used in every facet of organisational life, from learning activities to business planning processes, from personnel evaluations to client relations, from stakeholder management to communication, from process design to implementation. In some situations the different types of Inclusion Nudges should be used together or as a follow-up to obtain the needed effect. Motivation acquired through a "FEEL THE NEED" Inclusion Nudge might call for a "PROCESS" Inclusion Nudge to support behavioural change or alter the organisational culture.

Everyone can learn to design Inclusion Nudges. We believe that if all internal agents of organisational change master these techniques, our actions and behaviours will better leverage the full potential of all people, thereby producing more successful organisations.

Context on the Inclusion Nudges in this Guidebook

The Inclusion Nudges shared in this Guidebook were not tested in academic research settings but in real situations in organisations from all sectors. As authors, we have not evaluated the submitted Inclusion Nudges based on quantitative or qualitative data. The Guidebook is founded on trust that the examples our peers shared have worked, either in their organisations or in others.

Distinguishing between an effective practice and an Inclusion Nudge is not always simple. In fact, several submissions to this Guidebook described programmes or actions that could be successfully implemented as part of a strategic focus on topics such as inclusion, diversity, equity, wellbeing and agile

© T. Nielsen & L. Kepinski, 2016
www.inclusion-nudges.org

working, or as follow-up activities to make the priority stick. While these practices, often far-reaching and complex, are in line with current I&D work, they qualify as Inclusion Nudges only if they target the subconscious decision-making process. In some cases, Inclusion Nudges might be found *within* these good practices, and we have included a few of these examples in this Guidebook. We thank all the contributors for their submissions.

We recognize that it is not easy to bring to the surface what happens on an automatic, unconscious level. It requires knowledge of how our brains work and why we act as we do. Within an organisation it requires both a partnership among key decision makers and willingness on the part of the change agent to explore, inquire, and experiment. The following sections offer examples of the three types of Inclusion Nudges from the authors and from contributors around the world. We hope they will inspire you in your own experimentation with Inclusion Nudges.

Section 3: EXAMPLES OF "FEEL THE NEED" INCLUSION NUDGES

Reminder:

This type of Inclusion Nudge is focused on motivating people by making them feel the need for change rather than only having a rational understanding of the need for systemic and behavioural change.

Inspirational Thoughts

"Emotions...are like perceptions and memories – they are reconstructed from the data at hand. Much of that data comes from your unconscious mind as it processes environmental stimuli picked up by your senses and creates a physiological response. The brain also employs other data, such as your pre-existing beliefs and expectations, and information about the current circumstances. All of that information is processed, and a conscious feeling of emotion is produced." – **Leonard Mlodinow**

"Emotions play an important role in people's decision making, and behavioural economics incorporates this important fact of life into its decision theory.... In fact, research has shown that people who suffer damage to the emotional part of the brain are no longer able to engage in rational decision making." – **Morris Altman**

"Reason and emotion are not separate and opposed. Reason is nestled upon emotion and dependent upon it. Emotion assigns value to things, and reason can only make choices on the basis of those valuations." – **David Brooks**

"There are a variety of ways that emotional processes affect reason in a nuanced way... [for example,] just the simple tendency to experience an emotion, can actually...shape beliefs over time." – **David Pizarro**

Inspirational Thoughts *Continued*

"People pay more attention to personal appeals to act than impersonal [rational] ones…. Most of us have an intuitive reaction against [impersonal appeals]. To avoid that intuitive reaction, [we] need to do something different, something that's good practice anyway: be authentic and personal. " – **Stephen Wendel**

"The heart-vs.-head metaphor is an oversimplification, but nevertheless reflects a deep truth about human decision making. … Emotions exert pressure on behaviour. They are, in short, automatic processes that tell us what to do…. Reason cannot produce good decisions without some kind of emotional input, however indirect." – **Joshua Greene**

"FEEL THE NEED" Inclusion Nudge:

ILLUSTRATE BIASED EVALUATION & SELECTION OF CANDIDATES

Submitted by: Tinna C. Nielsen, Founder of Move the Elephant for Inclusiveness;
Howard Ross and Leslie Traub, Cook Ross Inc.[21]

Why

The same behaviour or performance is rated differently due to gender, appearance, name, skin colour, etc. Mitigate biases and get managers motivated to change ways of evaluating people to make more objective evaluations and select the best candidate.

The Inclusion Nudge

Use an evaluation exercise with different candidates but 100% identical resumes and narratives and only pictures, names, gender, skin colour as the differentiators. Leaders evaluate one candidate each, ratings are compared in plenary, patterns identified. The inclusion nudge is when showing the leaders the results and telling them that all candidates are 100% identical except the pictures and identity dates. Purpose is to show instead of tell managers that their evaluation and selection decisions are biased regardless of their rational belief that they evaluate candidates based on objective criteria. The Inclusion Nudge illustrates the result and consequences of their decisions instead of rationally trying to convince leaders that they are biased.

How

This exercise can be used in training sessions, leadership programmes, when presenting an I&D business case, to get buy-in and commitment for change in the recruitment process.

- Write a short, fictional description of a relevant position in your organisation.

- Create one fictional "candidate" but use different names, gender or pictures. You can create various versions of this Inclusion Nudge, such as:
  - Use a real application from a woman in your organisation who is qualified for the position (or merge applications from several successful women) and make a version using a male name.
  - Use the resume of a successful existing employee (with his or her permission) and create a narrative about the person's career. For ideas on how to write this narrative, see the Heidi Roizen case study from Harvard Business School.
  - Arla also uses an exercise designed by Cook Ross Inc. called "The Big Decision™". A resume and narrative with different names, gender, and photos. For information, please contact Cook Ross Inc.[22]

- Instruct the leaders to rate one of the candidates using the same method as in the company's recruitment processes – for example, a 1-5 scale. Instruct them to rate how likely they are to hire or promote this candidate. If you use only two versions with a man and a woman, ask them to rate how qualified they find the candidate, if they would want to collaborate with him/her, and if they would hire him/her.

- Show them the results of the ratings for all the candidates together, and point out how much the ratings deviate. Then reveal that the candidates are identical except for gender. Involve participants in spotting patterns in the ratings, such as gender and race/ethnicity differences. Facilitate a discussion about the impact of the implicit norms for performance and leadership in the organisation. Present research studies illustrating various cognitive biases.

- Facilitate a dialogue about the implicit associations, stereotypes and consequences in hiring and, more broadly, in terms of business strategy. Ask leaders what they will do to ensure better evaluations and choices. Introduce them to some of the "PROCESS" Inclusion Nudges focusing on recruitment, to give them some enablers that support the motivation (created with this "FEEL THE NEED" Inclusion Nudge) to change behaviour.

INCLUSION NUDGES

Practical Techniques for Behaviour, Culture, & System Change to Mitigate Unconscious Bias &
Create Inclusive Organisations

- Recommend the leaders to take some of the Implicit Association Test to spot their biases[23]. Inform them that seeing own behavioural patterns (incl. biases) helps the brain change behaviour.

Impact

This Inclusion Nudge is an eye-opener for participants and the majority is surprised about the results when hearing about the process/exercise design. The exercise motivates managers and recruiters to alter behaviour in people-evaluation processes and to change the process in order to make hiring choices based on the right competencies rather than on unconscious bias. At Arla sites, this has resulted in implementing various Inclusion Nudges and practices, such as diverse recruiting teams, interview in two parts, not look at identity data that mitigate bias in the process. The majority of hiring managers refer to this exercise/experience in recruiting processes to ensure a continuous focus on bias.

Authors' Comments

This Inclusion Nudge targets:
1. Behavioural drivers (in this case, overconfidence in our own rationality and processing of information).
2. Biases (negative and positive) for gender, name, religion, race, appearance, etc.

"FEEL THE NEED" Inclusion Nudge:

VERBALISING UNCOMFORTABLE BIASED INTERACTIONS

Submitted by: Vernā Myers, Vernā Myers Consulting Group

Why

Unconscious bias is deeply ingrained in how we interact with others. Awareness is a critical first step in mitigating its effects. It can feel uncomfortable to acknowledge bias, both to ourselves and to others, either in the moment or when reflecting on past situations. However, if we don't first acknowledge bias, the process of changing our behaviour can be stalled. To make progress, we need to become more comfortable with and skilled in these discussions.

The Inclusion Nudge

Saying *"ouch"* or *"awkward"* at the right moment allows you to interrupt the problematic behaviour even if you don't know why it's uncomfortable or offensive.

How

- We created an online experience where users push a button labelled *"awkward"* when they see a person or scene that is biased or creates exclusion.
- In our workshops and conversations, we suggest people say *"ouch"* when others say something that strikes them the wrong way.
- In real life, we suggest the same: saying *"ouch"* or *"awkward"* allows you to interrupt the problematic behaviour even if you don't know why it's uncomfortable or offensive.

Impact

Even if the bias is unclear, you are able to create a pause or share some feedback in a situation where the offensive behaviour would otherwise continue uninterrupted.

Authors' Comments

This is an example of a seemingly simple, yet effective, way to interrupt automatic thinking...making the unexamined visible. Of course, it requires self-reflection, becoming more aware of our emotional or "gut" reactions to situations, and a commitment to follow through with examining what was "awkward". This can be a powerful basis for behaviour interruption and change. In a sense, this is a "FEEL THE NEED" Inclusion Nudge that we do to ourselves.

"FEEL THE NEED" Inclusion Nudge:

SPOTLIGHT LACK OF DIVERSITY VISIBILITY IN INTERNAL COMMUNICATION

Submitted by Jolanda Verbeek, Diversity & Inclusion Manager, Royal Dutch Shell

Why

Despite a high past level of leadership support for D&I in the company, there was less visibility in recent times. Employees noticed this. Leaders did not. A need to get leaders engaged & motivated to put more focus on I&D.

The Inclusion Nudge

Show the actual pictures of people used in company communications. Illustrate the patterns (demographic, functional, and hierarchical) of who is visible or invisible. Make an eye-opener that illustrate that those being visible in communication were not representative of the workforce (internal and external).

How

Conduct D&I analysis of news items on the company Intranet (corporate home page and business units' home pages) from i.e. the past three months, noting:

- Gender (or other demographic differences) of employees referred to in news items

- Gender of employees featured in images in news items

- Instances of employees being referred to in news articles by gender, job level or business function

Prepare summary and share with leaders. Illustrate/show the patterns instead of showing just numbers.

© T. Nielsen & L. Kepinski, 2016
www.inclusion-nudges.org

Impact

- Senior leaders were surprised by the lack of visibility of Inclusion & Diversity in communications. They have become more visible on D&I leadership, individually and collectively.

- A guide was developed for internal and external communications providing an Inclusion & Diversity lens on content.

- Employees' perception of the importance of Inclusion & Diversity to the company increased.

Authors' Comments

This simple inclusion nudge counters perceptions with realities. There is a bias where people tend to recall the past as more positive and favourable than it was reported at the time. By showing images from past internal communications, Shell nudged leaders to more accurately recall the "real situation", thus motivating them toward engagement and change.

This Inclusion Nudges could be further developed by engaging the leaders asking them: "*How do you think reality is*?" and make their suggestions visible and then show/compare reality. Make it clear if there is a gap. That will work as an extra eye-opener.

"FEEL THE NEED" Inclusion Nudge:

HUMANISE AUDIT DATA TO CREATE BUY-IN FOR I&D INITIATIVES

The authors have merged several submissions due to similarities in approach and impact.

Submissions by: Josefine van Zanten, Royal DSM, SVP, ONE DSM Culture Agenda; Katrien Van Eetvelde, Senior HR Change Consultant, AXA Technology Services; Lisa Kepinski, Founder, Inclusion Institute

Why

Executive leaders may not be aware of the actual experiences of employees, especially those who are non-majority, within the organisation. In this context it is challenging to gain strong executive leadership commitment to culture change that will lead to sustainable progress.

The Inclusion Nudge

Humanise the data and numbers from organisational culture audits. Use real-life stories, vignettes, and quotes from employees as a way to generate motivation to support I&D initiatives more actively. Use these as a way to illustrate reasons for lack of progress of significant progress in Inclusion & Diversity.

How

Conduct an organisational scan/culture audit to provide a structured format for conveying employees' experiences with the organisation.

- Select a neutral, credible external partner to conduct confidential interviews of all executives and selected male and female employees. This helps ensure open dialogue for gathering real experiences that are not biased from an internal perspective.

- Have the independent consultant present the audit outcome to executives by using this Inclusion Nudge or the suggestion in 'Authors' comments'. Include non-identifying illustrative stories and actual quotes (anonymous) in the final report. This real-life story sharing helps humanise the rational data on the organisational culture.

- Hold a session for executives on unconscious bias using other inclusion nudges to show – not tell – the impact of biases, helping them feel the need to make changes. Follow with discussion on where bias may be turning up in their decisions and within the organisational culture. Discuss actions and what's needed from them for success.

Impact

Senior leaders tend to be more moved to commit to culture change when hearing stories, often surprising to them, of their employees' experiences in the organisation. Katrien gained support for rolling out UB training and a reciprocal mentoring program. Josefine gained support for the I&D strategy and actions. Lisa gained support for gender initiatives and agile working initiative.

Authors' Comments

Rather than just telling the executives that *"This is what's needed"* and doing it (often with limited executive engagement), this approach brings the voice of the employee into the discussion in a safe way. Executives deal with data and numbers constantly. This over-reliance on seemingly "rational" input and decision making can lead to an approach that may be overlooking emotions in favour of a seemingly "rational" decision making style. These stories move beyond only the "rational" data, and hit on the emotional level of the subconscious and trigger stronger commitment to the subsequent initiatives. They use the whole brain for commitment. You can make this intervention even more powerful by not using PowerPoint, but print the quotes and post them on the walls of the conference room (illustrate the message) and ask the leaders to walk around and read them.

"FEEL THE NEED" Inclusion Nudge:

SHOW HOW GROUP DYNAMICS REDUCE DIVERSE PERSPECTIVES

Submitted by: Veronika Hucke, D&I Strategy & Solutions

Why

Leaders regularly struggle to understand that a focus on increasing diversity benefits the whole organization rather than just minority groups. There tends to be little awareness of group dynamics that often suppress different opinions being voiced in a homogenous team, thus impacting the quality of decision making and performance. The impression that it is "good for them" rather than "good for the organization" can lead to a limited level of support for inclusion & diversity (I&D) measures thus impacting outcomes.

The Inclusion Nudge

Conduct an exercise in a team meeting or training session to illustrate how the quality of decision making is affected by group dynamics as people conform to what the majority of group members think, thus showing why diversity and inclusiveness benefit all of them.

How

- Select one of the Asch Conformity Experiment videos on YouTube[24].
- Depending on group size:
    - Use the video in a group meeting as the starting point for an I&D discussion, a project group launch, or a business planning session. Ask participants to work in pairs to share their impression and whether they can relate to the situation. Ask them to share back with the group. This approach works better in smaller groups.

    - if the group is big or your are not sure that someone will step forward and share a personal experience, send the link ahead of time and set up an anonymuos survey asking whether people recognize the situation and have conformed to group think themselves.

- Facilitate a discussion on the impact of and actions needed to increase inclusion and diversity. This tends to be much easier, as the team realizes that changes not only benefit people "who are different", but each individual team member. (See also the "PROCESS" Inclusion Nudge from Tinna C. Nielsen on how to reduce conformity in groups in order to leverage diverse perspectives.)

Impact

This inclusion nudge creates the basis for a totally different kind of dialogue, as team members share how they are holding back. It is a quick and simple way to shift the discussion since everybody tends to recognize the situation.

"FEEL THE NEED" Inclusion Nudge:

ADDRESS FEAR OF GENDER INITIATIVES

Submitted by: Axel Jentzsch, BASF, Diversity + Inclusion, European Manager

Why

Some senior leaders overestimated the effect of setting internal targets for women in leadership positions and thus had a negative reaction to the idea; "no chances for white male middle-class employees".

The Inclusion Nudge

Illustrate with a visual image the current representation of women and men in the company as compared with the proposed increase due to the company's internal targets for gender representation.

How

- In talent development discussions, show a slide with 100 figures, some male, some female, coloured slightly differently in order to make the difference more visible. The gender percentages should match the real situation in that unit/company.
- Show a similar, second slide with a few more female figures than the first slide, matching the target numbers for the unit/company.
- Switch back and forth between these two slides, asking, *"Do you see the difference?"* Managers perceive the small number of women only after a while, and it takes even longer to perceive the increase in women on the second slide.

Impact

This Inclusion Nudge helps managers put into perspective the fear of losing development opportunities for men, and leads to:

- Motivation to put more emphasis on the development of women
- Realise these changes will not reduce their opportunities

   © T. Nielsen & L. Kepinski, 2016

INCLUSION NUDGES

Practical Techniques for Behaviour, Culture, & System Change to Mitigate Unconscious Bias &
Create Inclusive Organisations

Authors' Comments

This Inclusion Nudge is a simple but effective solution that targets a key – and rather common – root cause for resistance to I&D work. It helps "shrink the change" so the fear factor is reduced. The impact of the change is thus perceived more objectively, which can reduce resistance. With this Inclusion Nudge, managers are able to more easily overcome their fears and get on board when they see the illustration of the *relatively small increase* as compared to the total population of employees. This capitalizes on the human motivational driver of *it's easier to commit to a smaller change*.

"FEEL THE NEED" Inclusion Nudge:

CHALLENGE "SPLIT SECOND" INTERPRETATIONS

Submitted by: Suzanne Price, Founder of Price Global

Why

Despite a mandate for a diverse slate of candidates for job openings, for two years there was no change in the talent pipeline with regard to gender and no increase in the number of women and Asians in senior positions. (This was a European company located in Asia Pacific). There is a need to reduce bias in talent development as well as in interview and selection processes

The Inclusion Nudge

Using an interactive exercise, illustrating the power of split-second interpretations of people and how these can vary based on very little information. Link these often surprising insights to the impact in interview situations.

How

- Deliver a workshop/session on unconscious bias in selection processes.

- Include a slide with six or seven pictures of fictional candidates, representing differences in gender, age, ethnicity and race, as well as different body language and clothing.

- Separate participants into groups and ask them to discuss which candidates they would hire, based on the information they have so far.

- After some time for discussion, announce there is more information and show a second slide with speech bubbles for each candidate. Include some that may be outside the traditional expectation such as: an Asian male saying, "I am a single father"; a Caucasian woman saying, "I am fluent in Mandarin"; an Asian saying, "People expect me to speak the language but I can't". Other ideas might include "My parents expect me home by 7pm", "I want an international assignment" and so on.

- Allow groups to continue discussing their choices of candidates.

- During the debriefing, ask: What impacted their decisions? Did anyone change their view once they saw the additional information? Did anyone manage to change someone else's mind? If so, how?

- Parallel into a conversation around how we make split-second decisions about people and how this impacts what we say to them, how we treat them etc.

- Ask them how they will challenge this – what kind of interventions they will apply in daily actions and people evaluation sessions.

Impact

- The exercise created support and buy-in from leaders to promote this kind of interventions in the organisation resulting in training on unconscious bias being delivered to hiring managers and HR employees using this exercise.

- Job interview processes were reviewed and changed to ensure diverse gender and ethnicity representation on the interview panel. Debriefing after interviews was introduced so the interview panel can share their views and challenge each other on any apparent bias in their assessments of the candidates.

Authors' Comments

This Inclusion Nudge could with benefits be used as part of an existing organisational process such as a people calibration process. It is our experience as internal I&D practitioners that mitigating bias and ensuring inclusive decision making has a bigger impact when the intervention is part of the actual choice process instead of merely workshops and training sessions.

"FEEL THE NEED" Inclusion Nudge:

ILLUSTRATING BIASED JUDGEMENTS AND BEHAVIOURAL IMPLICATIONS

Submitted by: Howard Ross, Founder & Chief Learning Officer, and Leslie Traub, Chief Consulting Officer, Cook Ross Inc. (original design)[24]
Modified European design by Tinna C. Nielsen, Founder of Move the Elephant for Inclusiveness, and Lisa Kepinski, Founder, Inclusion Institute

Why

Biased, usually unconscious, judgments of others (both of individuals and across social groups such as "women" or "Asians", etc.) are made within nanoseconds, often triggered by someone's gender, appearance, name, skin colour, accent, etc. This has an impact on our interactions in terms of feelings and level of engagement with others. In the workplace, this is especially problematic when we make hiring decisions and when we assess the talent and potential of others. Because most people have intentions to treat others fairly and also have a firm belief in the meritocracy of their organisation, it can be very hard to see and accept that one is making biased judgments of others.

The Inclusion Nudge

Use an exercise with pictures and description of real people to show, instead of tell managers, that their decisions, leadership, and interactions with people are biased regardless of their rational belief that they see all people objectively. This Inclusion Nudge illustrates the result and consequences of snap judgment and decisions instead of rationally trying to convince leaders that they are biased.

How

- Familiarize yourself with the research on "Warmth vs Competency" by Cuddy, Fiske, & Glick, 2007. Visit Amy Cuddy's research publications site where you can find many of her articles on biases and judgments of social groups.[25]
- Collect material for creating an exercise which highlights how quickly we judge others on warmth (likeability) and competency (performance).

- o Collect photos of about 6-10 *real* people about which you can also find out some facts. These may be people in the public sphere or people that you know who have given you permission to use their image and information. *Customize* this exercise to your organisation and the people who will be participating in the exercise.
  - ▪ Include some people who could touch upon some of the biases that are prevalent in your organisation. For example, if there is a bias against older employees, seek out a photo of someone who looks older, or a bias against people with body piercing, then seek a photo of someone with this in their appearance.
  - ▪ Get a mix of people that could potentially trigger *positive* and *negative* biases.
- o Gather a few facts about each of the people that you will use in the exercise. These may cover their education, professional accomplishments, descriptions from notable people about the person in the photo, press headlines from stories about the person, and quotations from the person herself or himself. Include facts that may be a surprise about the person, such as a person with body piercings is also a very well-respected leader in a multinational corporation and has an MBA from a leading university, or a person with a wide smile and open facial expression is actually a convicted felon and in prison for life.
- o Also, if possible, get a few other images that may show the person in another light (example smiling and frowning, or informal and formal clothes, etc.) to illustrate the difference appearance or context have on evaluations

- **Build the exercise:**
  - o Place one photo of each person on a slide (one person per slide). Number the slides, 1, 2, 3… in large font so it's easy for all to see the slide number. Nothing else is on the slides.
  - o Create a one page hand-out for the participants which has a table with three columns: the first is labelled "*Slide Number*", the second is labelled "*Warmth*" and the third column is labelled "*Competent*". You can also add a fourth column labelled "Would you actively seek this person out for knowledge sharing or collaboration?". In rows

under the "*Slide Number*" column, have the slide numbers recorded (1, 2, 3 …). Leave the other 2 columns blank for the participants to complete. Insert instructions on the hand-out "*Rate the person you see on Warmth and Competency using a rating scale of 1 to 5, with 1 being the lowest and 5 being the highest.*" Adjust the rating scale if used differently in your country (i.e. 1 is the highest and 5 is the lowest), or if in a multi-national group, make sure to include a definition on the rating scale as this varies across cultures.

o   Create another slide with all photos used, lined up with the photo and the slide number next to its respective photo.

o   Finally, create a slide for each person shown in the photos and add in one or two other photos of him or her showing other appearance or context, their name, occupation and/or what they are most known for, and a few surprising facts about the person.

- **Conduct the exercise:**
    o   Introduce the participants briefly to the research on Warmth and Competence – how we scan and evaluate people unconsciously and why we do this as human beings.

    o   Explain to the participants that they are to do the first part of this exercise in silence. They will see a series of photos of people and they will have 5-10 seconds to look at the photo. They should then record their own assessment on the person's warmth (likeability) and competency (performance) using the scale given. Remind them to not talk during this part of the exercise.

    o   Show each of the slides with the single photo; 5-10 seconds per slide. Have a blank slide or cover the projector to give a few moments of pause for the participants to record their assessments of the people on the hand-out. Proceed this way through all people photos.

    o   Now show the slide with all the photos and invite them to look for patterns as you go through each picture and information on who these people are.

    o   Reveal who the people really are by showing the slides with their photos, name, and information about them. Ask participants, "*What did you notice?*", "*Who did you rate high on warmth?*", "*… low on warmth?*", "*… high on competency?*", "*… low on* *competency?" "Who would you want on your work team?" "... as a neighbour?", "... as a boss?"* Discuss why there can be so many different views of the same people. Also inform them about the global norms the research (and the experience you build up doing this exercise in many settings) have identified, i.e. elderly high on warmth and low on competency, obese low on competency, and Asians low on warmth and high on competency. Discuss the implications for the workplace, people and business

o   Link to the Cuddy, Fiske, & Glick, 2007 research on warmth and competency and how various social groups are rated, as well as the behavioural implications.

o   Facilitate a dialogue about the implicit associations, stereotypes, biases, and consequences in the workplace and marketplace for judgements that we make of others. Link to the business strategy and people talent systems and processes. Ask leaders what they will do to ensure biased evaluations are noticed and mitigated. Explore what Inclusion Nudges could be created within the systems and processes.

Impact

- This Inclusion Nudge is an eye-opener to most people and it motivates managers and employees to monitor their judgments of people, and it provides a platform for open discussions on unconscious bias.

- In Arla Foods this exercise is used in the leadership training, as well as in team sessions by the HR professionals and managers. It is also an integrated part of the people calibration process, where it is used in the calibration meetings to make the bias discussions more present and related to real candidates. New pictures are being applied regularly to fit the context.

- Several of the managers in Arla Foods have made a similar template on warmth and competence that they use to rate candidates in recruitment and promotion processes. They use their ratings to discuss in the recruiting panel how these snap judgments affect their evaluation of performance.

- A similar process can be imbedded into any talent management process by using pictures of the person being evaluated, mentored, etc. and having the supervisor notice their warmth and/or competence assessments

Authors' Comments:

In the future, we hope to hear of some "PROCESS" Inclusion Nudges which have been designed as a result of this "FEEL THE NEED" Inclusion Nudge.

"FEEL THE NEED" Inclusion Nudge:

SPOTLIGHTING BIASED CUSTOMER-CLAIM HANDLING

Submitted by: Anonymous[26]

Why

Most employees think they make decisions about client/customer claims in an objective, rational way, based on the data/merits of each individual case. The challenge is to help employees be aware of the potential for biased decision-making when they interact with clients/customers.

The Inclusion Nudge

This exercise highlights biased perceptions of customers through visualisation and reflection, and interjects more objectivity (a fresh start) in future interactions with the same or "similar" customers.

How

The exercise is done at the beginning of a workshop for employees who interact with clients/customers and also make financial decisions on behalf of the company according to contractual agreements with clients/customers.

- Ask employees to think about a claim they have processed in the past that was for a particularly difficult client who was awkward, unreasonable or even rude.

- Then, ask each one to tell the group about their example, concentrating on describing the client's characteristics rather than the technical details of the claim. In order to bring unconscious bias to the surface, you may have to prompt them with questions such as *"What nationality was the client? What accent did they have?"*, etc.

- Next, ask them to imagine that the client is standing in front of them about to make another claim. *"How would they feel? How would they react? How would this influence their decision-making process about the new claim?"*

- Finally, ask them to imagine a new client with the same characteristics as the *"difficult"* one, and reflect on how they would feel about the new client's claim.

Impact

The Inclusion Nudge ensures that each client's claim is adjusted based on more objective and rational data. The employee is less vulnerable to influence from similar past experiences.

Authors' Comments

This Inclusion Nudge is effective in surfacing the implicit associations we project on to people and interfere with objective/professional client service – without having to lecture about this. The Inclusion Nudge has potential of being further developed by *illustrating* the hidden patterns in customer claims (if such data is available) – for example, the link between the outcome of claim handling and the characteristics of the customer, i.e. gender, nationality, age. The key intervention is to illustrate the biases, not just show the numbers. This could be done by putting claims on the wall and clustering them in gender, ethnicity, generation etc. This kind of intervention has been proven to be very powerful in terms of motivating for change because of the *"aha-effect"* of seeing the scale of the problem.

"FEEL THE NEED" Inclusion Nudge:

REAL-LIFE SCENARIOS TO SHIFT BEHAVIOURS AND COMMITMENT

Submitted by: Carol Putnam, Ph.D., Thrive Coaching

Why

Spotlight for top managers where unconscious bias, inappropriate behaviours and disciplinary actions are occurring. The challenge is to raise awareness across the top 50 leaders and engage them in problem identification and actions.

The Inclusion Nudge

This exercise spotlights actual scenarios occurring in the organisation.

How

The company president began the session by sharing his distress and disappointment about what he had been made aware of over the past year. He said he wanted all the leaders to look closely at the scenarios and answer three questions:

- *Do we have a systemic problem?*
- *What as a leadership team do we need to do differently?*
- *What will they personally do differently going forward?*

The leaders, working in teams, were shocked by the scenarios. Some didn't believe the scenarios were real or that they were representative of senior leaders in the organisation.

Incorporate these steps:

- Before the session, meet with the senior leader to discuss the need for awareness across the leadership team of inappropriate behaviours and the culture they create.
- Develop scenarios based upon real situations.
- Develop questions to spark conversations regarding the scenarios.
- Provide talking points to the senior leader for the kick-off of the session.

- Mix up the teams for the discussion. Each team should receive a different scenario.
- Have each team describe the scenario to the group, noting salient points, their key questions and areas of discussion.
- Ask participants to develop an action plan for their units and for themselves as leaders.

Impact

Each leader made a commitment to confront inappropriate behaviours, coach their teams and shift the culture. Many then replicated the process with their leadership teams in conjunction with their HR business partner.

Authors' Comments

This could be very useful for all situations in which one is trying to make the invisible, visible. This Inclusion Nudge is effective because it targets feelings of empathy, surprise, disgust, and exclusion. When we experience others being excluded, the area of the brain where we feel physical pain is activated. Emotional triggers have been proven to motivate behavioural change.

"FEEL THE NEED" Inclusion Nudge:

RAISE THE COMFORT LEVEL WITH DISABILITIES

Submitted by: Anonymous

Why

Many people have no experience of working side-by-side with people with different abilities. This often leads to bias such as regarding a person with a disability as totally incapable of working. This is a key challenge in including persons with disabilities in a workplace.

The Inclusion Nudge

Create eye-opener interventions that counter assumptions about people with disabilities by designing exercises and work initiatives that team up people with and without disabilities.

How

Create an interactive session or workshop for a team that includes people with disabilities.

- Form a team of fewer than 30 people.

- Invite people with disabilities as lecturers who can explain and demonstrate their different abilities and experiences, such as:
    - Blind person who can read texts faster than average seeing people if equipped with screen-reader software
    - Blind person who has no problem writing/reading e-mail
    - Deaf person with better dynamic vision in a wider range
    - Deaf person who can focus well at work because they are not disturbed by sounds
    - People with disabilities are often creative and have good problem-solving skills

- People with disabilities can help you look at the environment from different perspectives

- Ask participants to visualise their day as a person with disability, beginning with waking up in the morning, and figure out how they would manage if they had a certain kind of disability.

- Lead a group discussion focusing on topics such as: what they felt or thought during the presentation, the comfort/discomfort of working together, their perceptions of people with disabilities prior to and after the session/initiatives.

Impact

Being taught by a person with a disability is a paradigm shift for people who unconsciously believe that people with disabilities are to be helped or taught. People witness capabilities of those with disabilities, thus raising their comfort level with including people with disabilities in their workplace.

"FEEL THE NEED" Inclusion Nudge:

REALISING THE BENEFITS OF BLIND INTERVIEWS

Submitted by: Gina Badenoch, Founder of Ojos que Sienten (Charity) and
Capaxia Consultancy Firm

Why

Through 9 years of working with blind people teaching them photography, it
became clear that many sighted people suffer from "mental blindness" created
by their prejudices and stereotypes. We label people, objects and situations very
quickly using visual cues. What happens when you talk to someone and see them
later, for the first time? Could we actually make better decisions about people
without seeing them?

The Inclusion Nudge

Blind job interview. During the beginning of the interview the interviewers
cannot see the candidate.

How

The blind interviews have been done in two different versions in the
organisations where is has been applied. The interviewers conduct the interview
behind a screen or with their back turned to the candidate during the beginning
of the interview.

Next time you have the opportunity to interview somebody for a job at your
company, try receiving them with your chair turned in the opposite direction to
the candidate. Then carry out the first five minutes of the interview without
seeing them. This will no doubt be uncomfortable for both parties. However, it
creates an opportunity to listen to the person and to form opinions without
prejudging them from sight.

Make sure to prepare the candidates by letting them know in advance that when
they walk into the room there will be people (more than one to balance the bias
each person may have and have a diverse group of interviews) sitting with their

back towards the entrance or behind a screen. Tell them the purpose is to help outsmart our unconscious bias.

After the first five minutes of the blind interview, ask the candidate if there's anything they would like to say before moving forward with the rest of the interview. At the end of the interview ask for their comments from the experience. Also get the comments from the interview team.

Impact

The person being interviewed usually feels slightly awkward, initially but quickly becomes more relaxed about answering questions when not seen. Their answers are usually more reflective of how they really think as opposed to giving an answer the interviewer wants to hear.

The person or team conducting the interview usually find that they concentrate much more on what the candidate is saying rather than visual aspects during the interaction.

This is part of an inclusive process that humanises the way people can identify talent. It is part of levelling the playing field!

Authors' Comments

While this example is similar to the 'PROCESS' Inclusion Nudge on Blind Interviews, we have included this one as it raises an 'a-ha' factor by realising the benefits of blind interviews. It can be a great first step before an organisation is willing to fully commit to the entire interview being in a blind process.

"FEEL THE NEED" Inclusion Nudge:

SEE THE IMPORTANCE OF DIVERSE CONSUMERS

Submitted by: Kevin Bradley, Sr. Manager D&I, Discover Financial Services
Source of inspiration: Gerry Fernandez, Executive Director, Multicultural
Foodservice and Hospitality Alliance

Why

During D&I work, questions can arise about the value of diversity in the
marketplace or the actual business impact of Inclusion & Diversity. *"If I make a
quality product, doesn't it speak for itself? Why do I have to go after diverse
customers?"*

The Inclusion Nudge

Create visual example of the loss experienced by not having diverse customers.

How

Show participants a stack of money and ask them to pretend that this is their
business's cash drawer at the end of the night. Tell them that one of the dollars
came from a Hispanic customer, one from a disabled customer, one from an
African-American customer, one from a Caucasian customer, one from a single
mom, one from a gay couple, and so on.

Then ask them three questions:
1. *Do you know which dollar came from which customer?*
2. *Do you really care?*
3. *Which of these dollars do you want to "leave on the table" on a
   daily basis for your competitors to grab?*

Impact

This shows participants they are *"leaving money on the table."* People can *"get
it"* with their head, heart or wallet. This potentially impacts one or more of these
areas.

Authors' Comments

This very simple Inclusion Nudge is powerful because it taps into the loss aversion bias. Human beings are twice as miserable about losing something as they are happy about gaining the same thing. Thus triggering a feeling of loss is highly motivational for behavioural change. It is also possible to add to this Inclusion Nudge by asking the leaders to make a reversed business case with estimates on what the organisation is losing in revenue by continuing business as usual.

"FEEL THE NEED" Inclusion Nudge:

ILLUSTRATING GENDER GAP BY BENCHMARKING COMPETITORS

Submitted by: Anonymous

Why

Get top leaders to understand gender gaps inside the company.

The Inclusion Nudge

Use simple graphics to illustrate internal gender gaps compared to female representation at the leadership level among competitors. Make it easy to see the need for change.

How

Benchmark internal gender gaps with gender gaps of competitors or customers.

- Gather information from public sources (annual reports, CSR reports, and websites) about competitors' and customers' leadership teams. Include the executive committee and two or three levels below the CEO, as well as total workforce. Collect the same information for your company.

- Translate the information into a percentage of women at each level.

- Following the example below, create a table with a line for each competitor/customer and draw an X-axis at the bottom labelled percentage of women.

- Use a different colour for each company and graph the percentage of women at each level. Use a large female image to represent the highest percentage and a small female image for the lowest.

- Reorder the companies according to the gap sizes at each level.

- Group companies into those who leverage the women in their organisation and those who don't.

Impact

Top leaders realise where their company stands in terms of gender gap, which impacts how attractive it may be to female talents.

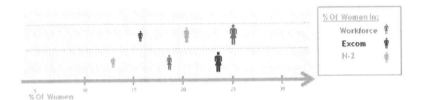

"FEEL THE NEED" Inclusion Nudge:

TESTING HYPOTHESIS ABOUT ORGANISATIONAL CULTURE

Submitted by: Alexa Mbowa, Organisational Effectiveness, Change and D&I Consultant

Why

Senior leaders lack awareness that the organisation's culture is becoming one of exclusion vs. inclusion. The challenge is to build insight about the lack of inclusion and create an imperative for collective action.

The Inclusion Nudge

Develop hypotheses about employees' perceptions of the organisational culture (focusing on the negative) in collaboration with senior leaders. Test these hypotheses in employee focus groups and report responses. This creates eye-openers and leads to a common sense of urgency for action.

How

- Alexa worked with the leadership to develop five hypotheses about what employees might be feeling about the culture. The hypotheses they agreed to as a team focused on the organisation's complexity, individuals' emotional connection, capacity for change, leadership visibility and recognition.

- They then co-designed (with Ipsos Loyalty, an independent employee research firm) half-day focus group sessions to test the leadership team's hypotheses. Note that they never specifically used the words Diversity & Inclusion (D&I) as they were faced with a legacy of stops and starts on the topic and needed a different angle. They also believed that real data on the D&I topic would be unearthed during the expert-led four-hour sessions. The approach they took was to make the FG sessions a critical element of their new "Creating a Great Place to Work" initiative.

 © T. Nielsen & L. Kepinski, 2016
www.inclusion-nudges.org

- The focus groups involved 11 sessions with 12-15 participants representing a cross-section of the employee population. Some participants were preselected (to ensure diversity) but the majority were volunteers. To create an environment in which employees felt safe to speak candidly, Ipsos facilitated the focus groups.

- Following the discussions, Ipsos captured the key themes and shared them with the leadership team. The data provided the leadership with undeniable evidence and eye-openers about the organisational culture and helped set the direction for creating a more inclusive environment.

- Alexa then worked with the leadership team to determine the way forward in a manner that took into account the diversity of the employee population. This included the development and implementation of a robust D&I strategy.

Impact

This approach developed common appreciation among the senior leadership, a sense of urgency for collective action and leadership accountability for culture change and the creation of a D&I strategy. As a result of this exercise, the leadership designed and championed an inspiring plan for change, which included a commitment to holding each other accountable for shifting the current culture.

"FEEL THE NEED" Inclusion Nudge:

TRIGGERING A REQUEST TO SPONSOR LGBT

Submitted by: Ben Capell, Organization Development Consultant and Scholar

Why

The company had a corporate LGBT inclusion statement, but in practise there was total silence around the issue. In many organisations the topic of LGBT inclusion is complicated due to the fact that it is not a visible diversity and because many people do not feel comfortable talking about it. The idea is to get HR and leaders to realize that their ownership is needed to promote a change. Break the silence around the topic of LGBT inclusion and integrate it as an HR priority.

The Inclusion Nudge

Simply ask senior managers to sponsor LGBT inclusion in the organisation, and to take an active role. The request itself triggers an emotional reaction and a realisation that the organisation is not as inclusive as they thought.

How

- Bring up the topic with HR managers/business partners (for example, when reviewing a business unit's I&D strategic plan or when discussing development opportunities for their business leaders). In many cases, expect to hear comments such as, *"I don't think there's an issue in our organisation/country."*

- Test this state with an action request: they need to recruit a senior executive in the company to speak about LGBT inclusion at an external or internal event or to be an LGBT Employee Resource Group executive sponsor.

- Follow up with the HR colleague. Typically, their experience has been one of multiple negative replies. This usually triggers a very different understanding of the situation for LGBT employees in the workplace. Through the request process, they have gained a new perspective on the type of exclusion and rejection that LGBT employees can feel in the workplace. They then become more committed to LGBT inclusion.

- Have them continue to help find leaders who are willing to learn about the topic, such as by inviting executives and HR to hear the experiences of some LGBT employees. This often gives HR colleagues and business leaders a greater understanding of LGBT experiences of exclusion. By hearing personal stories directly from LGBT employees in an open, honest format, they are usually moved emotionally and agree to become allies of the LGBT community.

Impact

The request process in itself triggered HR and senior executives to relate to the issues around exclusion of LGBT employees in their organisation and to agree to support change. Before this, there was a sense of "*no problem*".

"FEEL THE NEED" Inclusion Nudge:

APPOINTMENT TO HEAD DIVERSITY BOARD

Submitted by: Anonymous

Why

Some business units have very low female participation on the leadership team and leaders often don't *"see"* this. The majority (and privileged) are often blind to their own gender.

The Inclusion Nudge

The worst performing manager on gender balance in his business unit was asked to lead the diversity board by the CEO. Instead of pointing fingers or selecting the manager with the best gender balance as a role model, the one with the least representation was asked to take the lead.

How

- Statistics clearly showed that not all business units in the organisation had reasonable female participation in their management team.
- The CEO decided to create a diversity board and gave the role of leading it to the manager of the business unit with the worst gender balance.
- This newly appointed leader then had to create strategies and plans to improve diversity in the leadership.

Impact

This improved the gender balance in the company. The selected manager changed the mix of his leadership team so that at the end of his term his unit had the best gender balance in the leadership team. He explained that previously he did not think about gender when appointing people to his leadership team and did not interview any female candidates. After getting the role as leader for the diversity board, he thought actively about achieving a gender balance. More important, women stepped forward and made clear to him that they were interested in being part of the leadership team.

"FEEL THE NEED" Inclusion Nudge:

HUMANISE TALENT DATA TO GAIN SUPPORT FOR SPONSORSHIP INITIATIVE

Submitted by: Lisa Kepinski, Founder, Inclusion Institute

Why

Few women in top talent/successor pool and less visibility of women. Senior leaders knew less about the female talents than about the male talents in the senior executive pipeline. A sponsorship program was needed, but it was difficult to get support from senior leaders.

The Inclusion Nudge

A simple intervention/exercise to make the point that there was not gender equality within formal and informal networks and to reduce resistance to the need for greater visibility of women, thus encouraging sponsorship of female HiPo leaders.

How

- Before launching a sponsorship initiative for female senior talents, there was some resistance to the need for such a program. The executive leaders who were to be the sponsors felt that they advocated equally for men and women and that no special efforts were needed for women.

- The kick-off session began with a slide showing photos of all the employees at the female sponsorees' level, with men and women randomly mixed. More than 130 people were shown on one slide – tiny photos lined up in rows, but still visible when projected.

- When asked how many of these people they knew, the executives called out many names and could have gone on longer.

- Then came the next slide, which faded out the male photos, leaving only the few women. Asked again, *"How many of these people do you know?"* it turned out they knew only a small number.

Impact

The exercise removed much of the resistance of the executive leaders. They were much more willing to support the female sponsorship program. Within six months, a couple of women from this program were promoted. Also, there was greater cross-business and cross-geography discussion and visibility of these senior female talents.

Authors' Comments

This Inclusion Nudge if highly effective in showing the consequence of behavioural patterns/bias. It is also useful for illustrating national preferences, if there is a tendency that headquarters and upper/top leadership positions are dominated by one nationality (domestic).

"FEEL THE NEED" Inclusion Nudge:

SPONSORSHIP OF LEADERS OF NON-DOMINANT CULTURE GROUPS

Submitted by: Suzanne Price, Founder of Price Global

Why

Many senior executive committees lack diversity. There is a strong belief that *"we promote the best people for the job, we have a meritocracy"*.

The Inclusion Nudge

An exercise about sponsorship of people from dominant and non-dominant groups creates motivation for prioritising and engaging in sponsorship programs. The purpose is to raise awareness of the power associated with the dominant group and to inspire action to use this power on behalf of the non-dominant group to create more equitable organisations.

How

- Create a PPT slide showing three different people. Use colours, numbers or shapes to differentiate.

- Decide on one as the dominant success profile and the other two as less represented on the senior executive board.

- Put a cluster of people in a group to represent the executive committee: five from the dominant group, two from the less represented group and one from the least represented group.

- Underneath the boardroom table, put equal numbers of all groups mixed together.

- Ask participants if they were on the board at this company and it was time to select a new board member, whom would they chose – someone who belonged to the dominant group, the less dominant group and the least represented group.

- Take all answers and then ask, "*If you choose someone from the less represented group and they failed, how would that be perceived and how would that impact you*?" Then apply that to the other groups.

- It should become apparent that the dominant group is in a safer position to sponsor and promote underrepresented groups. Board members from underrepresented groups have extra pressure, if they extend a hand to others in their group, to make sure those people do not fail.

Impact

Resulted in introduction of sponsorship programmes for under-represented groups (women and Asians since this was in Asia-Pacific). Leaders from the dominant culture (white men in a U.S.-based multinational) acted as sponsors of talent from the non-dominant culture groups.

"FEEL THE NEED" Inclusion Nudge:

EXCHANGING PERSONAL EXAMPLES GAINING COMMITMENT TO CHANGE

Submitted by: Ben Capell, Organization Development Consultant and Scholar

Why

There was a clear need to get executives more personally and deeply involved in gender focus activities.

The Inclusion Nudge

A reverse session between executives and female leaders to create eye-openers for executives, where the women were instructed to tell personal experiences in work-life/career development and bring up issues that should be addressed and the executives were instructed to listen.

How

- Get senior leaders' agreement to discuss career development with female talent.

- Design the session as reverse mentoring: instead of preparing the women to hear a "speech", tell them this is their opportunity to ask questions and bring up topics that the senior leaders should address. At the same time, prompt the leaders to be in "listening mode".

- Create a cosy atmosphere where people can talk – small groups at round tables, no podium or slides.

- Prearrange a reflection session so that leaders can comment on what they learned. They are likely to express surprise and the need to change things.

- Facilitate the reflection session in a way that moves toward actions and monitoring. Get HR in the room.
- Make sure you do not close the session before you get personal commitments and book a follow-up session.

Impact

This reversed setting gave executives surprising insights into hidden barriers and enabled them to react quickly. There was much greater partnering of senior leaders with gender initiatives at the collective and personal level. Female employees got the chance to personally meet senior leaders for networking and sponsorship purposes.

"FEEL THE NEED" Inclusion Nudge:

SECURING LEADERSHIP ENGAGEMENT IN REDUCING HARASSMENT, BULLYING & DISCRIMINATION

Submitted by: Tinna C. Nielsen, Founder of Move the Elephant for Inclusiveness

Why

All organisations have incidences of unacceptable behaviour. Those who have not experienced it personally may find it difficult to grasp the impact. Internal statistics on harassment, bullying, mobbing and discrimination were not sufficient to trigger proactive measures on a systematic basis. Global action was needed to build the capabilities to address, handle and reduce unacceptable behaviour. To create buy-in and engagement from leaders/managers, it was necessary to make leaders, managers, and employees feel the need to address these problems and not just rationally understand the need.

The Inclusion Nudge

Display real-life and personal experiences from employees (with first person quotes) on a wall, have the leaders read them to feel the pain of their colleagues. Also show the reverse business case (the loss) of not changing the current state.

How

- **Collect real life examples**/personal experiences from the organisation: white collar, blue collar, leaders etc.

- Convert each example into **first-person quotes** like, *"When my colleagues go to lunch they never invite me. They often keep important information from me."*

- **Display these on the walls** in a meeting room (make sure to have enough or duplicate to cover a wall or more) and have leaders walk around in the room to read them.

- **Convert the *percentage*** of people who have experienced this behaviour (from internal employee survey) into an actual *number* of people (12% = xxxx employees in our organisation) going to work every day feeling miserable and underperforming as a result. Make this number visual: show, don't tell.

- **Make a *reverse business case*** ("FRAMING" Inclusion Nudge): show findings from research illustrating how much each person underperforms (e.g. 30% decrease in decision-making ability) or how one person in a team experiencing harassment affects the productivity of the team.

- Calculate and show how much the company loses financially (behavioural driver: losses have more weight more than gains).

- Show the most critical actions to take. Keep it simple and reduce complexity.

Impact

Top leaders were shocked by the real-life examples and by how these issues played out in their organisation. Some did not believe all of them; some said, "*This incident must be old – we fixed this years ago*". Some expressed discomfort and surprise. This Inclusion Nudge was used to engage other leaders in the organisation.

The result was immediate support. Resources were prioritised to take action immediately. The actions are to empower all leaders and employees to change this, and to strengthen the formal grievance and case-handling procedure to deal with critical situations.

"FEEL THE NEED" Inclusion Nudge:

TELLING EMPLOYEE'S STORIES FOR INCLUSION

Submitted by: Lisa Kepinski, Founder, Inclusion Institute.

Reviewed by Ann Dunkin, Senior Advisor, US Environmental Protection Agency

Sources of inspiration: first developed by Hewlett Packard GLEN (Gay & Lesbian Employees Network) Employee Resource Group, and then expanded to other diverse groups, including white men. Debbie Epstein, of Hewlett Packard, was also one of the originators of the Readers' Theatre.

Why

Often people are blind to exclusion and the micro behaviours that can cause the and how we all unintentionally contribute to some people feeling excluded and not valued by the company. Informing people about this will not change their behaviour – it is important to let them insights in personal real-life stories about this (target feelings).

The Inclusion Nudge

This is called "Reader's Theatre".

Real employee stories told by company employees/leaders to trigger deeper insight in the small behaviours that contribute to some people feeling excluded and others feeling included and valued by the company. The purpose is to highlight through personal stories the experience of exclusion and inclusion in the organisation and the impact this can have on the business; productivity, engagement, innovation, process improvement, company pride, talent retention and loyalty.

How

This was used with executives, managers and employees.

This is comprised of several short vignettes (in written form, less than one page each), both positive and negative, that employees have experienced. A variety of company employees (including senior managers and employees) are the readers.

© T. Nielsen & L. Kepinski, 2016
www.inclusion-nudges.org

- Collect the examples from employees and identify details are changed to protect employees.

- A collection of these, about 15, are then mixed to form the script of the "Reader's Theatre".

- A variety of company employees (including senior managers and employees) are the readers, with one or two stories assigned to each person. They do a couple of group practice reads to get comfortable with the story. All have a copy of the script in their hands, and they stand in a line in front of the audience.

- A moderator introduces the process ("*Stories will be read; these are true but the identifying details have been changed. Please listen in silence and note your own thoughts as you listen. A discussion will be held at the end of the Theatre*"). Then, the readers proceed with the stories, stepping forward when reading, stepping back when done, and so on.

- A discussion is facilitated afterwards: "*How did what you heard impact you? What is the impact on the employee? On the team? On the organisation? What would you do if this were you? Or your colleague? What is one take-away action that you will do going forward?*"

Impact

Having used this nudging technique for more than 15 years, I still hear back from people on how impactful it was in opening their thought process on the experiences of others. They also mention the quick checks they still do on their own behaviours which could further promote inclusion.

Authors' Comments

Anita Curle is a Global D&I learning and development lead in Shell, based in Calgary, Canada. She is also a contributor to the Inclusion Nudges Guidebook. In October 2015, Anita was designing a new D&I learning course for Shell and she wanted to use an exercise which effectively captured the attention of the participants on why D&I is important to

Shell and ensured their effective engagement in the subsequent workshop. Anita turned to the 'Feel the Need' examples in the Inclusion Nudges Guidebook and was inspired by this Readers' Theatre Inclusion Nudge. Anita reached out to Lisa to learn more about how it worked, and after discussion, Lisa also put Anita in contact with Debbie Epstein, her former colleague in Hewlett-Packard who was one of the original developers of the Readers' Theatre. Anita and Debbie discussed the exercise format and types of stories used in the past. In November, we heard back from Anita saying,

> *"I wanted to say a great big thank you for your guidance on the Readers' Theatre exercise. I delivered my pilot for my new course last Thursday. The Readers' Theatre stories helped get the participants "hearts and minds" into the topic and was a very powerful "nudge" to set up and start the workshop on inclusion!"*

We are pleased that Anita was inspired and created her version of this Inclusion Nudge to best suit her organisation. This is how we intended the Inclusion Nudges Guidebook to be used.

"FEEL THE NEED" Inclusion Nudge:

SEE TENDENCY TO HOMOGENEITY IN YOUR STRATEGIC INNER CIRCLE

Submitted by: Susanne Justesen, Ph.D. and Innovation Diversity Advisor, Innoversity Copenhagen

Why

We all have a group of people whom we will seek out for advice, when we face an important decision or have a difficult problem to solve. These may be peers across the organisation, or professional relations outside of the organisation. This strategic inner circle of our network usually consists of no more than 10 people, and could also be described as our professional (though un-official) advisory board. Unfortunately, most of us tend to seek help and advice from others who are very similar to ourselves. Research shows that we have a strong tendency to seek advice NOT from the most competent people within our network or organisation, but rather from the people that we like the most[27]. The consequence of this unfortunately is that too many people end up with very homogeneous advisory networks. And unfortunately, the more important our decision is, or the bigger and more complex our problem to be solved is, the larger the need for diversity amongst the people we trust. If we want to become better at innovative thinking and decision making, we need to make sure that we have a lot of different skill-sets and perspectives in our strategic inner circle. If we do not, this may end up having severe implications for our innovative potential as individuals and organisations.

The Inclusion Nudge

A quick assessment of your strategic inner circle to identify hidden patterns of similarities or differences to your own characteristics, such as age, function, gender, nationality, geography, company and other. Those people with 4 or more similarities to you will be crossed of the list and most people often having only 1 or 2 left. That is the surprising and motivational element in the Inclusion Nudge. This mini assessment of the quality of your strategic inner circle, will help you look at your own "advisory board" in a new way, by taking a closer and different look at the five people that you tend to seek out for help, advice, input on challenges in your professional job – to assess whether they tend to be very different or very similar to you, and to each other. What this mini-assessment does is to quickly test whether you tend to seek your input amongst similar others or amongst different others.

How

Use this assessment in a team session, workshop, training session, innovation group, ERG, etc.

- First: ask people to think of five people whom they like to seek out for help and advice on important PROFESSIONAL problems, challenges and decisions (these people are not their employees, but can be their spouse or best friend). Ask them to write the five names on a blank piece of paper

- Then (prepared in advance) hand out a table to each participant, with six (or more) horizontal rows + a header row and six vertical columns. The vertical columns have the following header titles: 1) Name, 2) Organisation, 3) Gender, 4) Educational background, 5) Age *(age difference from you in years +/-)*, and 6) Geographical distance *(distance from you in km/miles), and potentially other characteristics relevant for the group (i.e. sexual orientation, educational institution, headquarters)*. You can call the assessment something like; *"Who do you seek out for advice or input?"*

- Instruct the participants to write their own name in the first row and fill in their characteristics... (own name, name of organisation, gender, education, age, geographical location etc.)

- When they have filled out the first row with their own characteristics, then instruct the participants to take the five names which they just wrote on the blank piece of paper, and insert these five names below their own name, in the first column of the table.

- Then they take each name and fill out the row, while comparing their own "characteristics" with the characteristics of each person, based on whether they are different or similar. If they share the same characteristics, just make a (-), for instance if you belong to the same organisation, have the same age, educational background etc. Then just mark the space with (-). If you are different, write the difference (age difference: 4 years, or geographical distance 75 km, etc.).

- When they have done so for all five of their most important "advisors", instruct them to look at the table, and see if any of their most important 'advisors' share four or more of the same characteristics (marked with -)? If anyone on their list does so, instruct them to cross out the names of these advisors.

- When you instruct them to cross out the names of the very similar people, that is a very strong nudge, because when they have done so, you tell them that the reason you have asked them to cross out those particular names is, that the likelihood of these people to be able to tell you anything that you did not already know, or provide you with perspectives that you could not have come up with yourself, is very slim. So when you seek out this person for help, maybe you should ask yourself whether you are maybe more in search for support by someone who will agree with you. Good advice is much more likely to come from someone who is different from yourself.

Tinna C. Nielsen has facilitated this assessment (designed by S. Justesen) in Arla Foods for many years and has added:

- Instruct participants to also look for patterns of homogeneity in the vertical columns, such as does all 5 in the inner circle have the same gender, nationality, etc.

- Instruct the participants to discuss in small groups what each of them will do to challenge patterns of homogeneity (instruct them to use peer coaching – ask questions for reflection and not give advice)

Impact

Many people are really surprised to see how many people in their inner circle are very similarly thinking and therefore this seems as a powerful nudge for more diversity and inclusiveness to have people think differently about who to actively seek out for advice or input. Most people are surprised to have only a few people left on the list – only a few people that can potentially provide them with different perspectives that they would not have been able to come up with themselves.

This assessment is an eye-opener and motivates people to challenge an often hidden behavioural pattern and to actively reach out to other people they already trust and who can provide them with more diverse perspectives. The majority of the people having done this assessment report having changed behaviour and diversified their inner circle.

Authors' Comments

This Inclusion Nudge can also be used in people evaluation and selection processes*, to make our unconscious bias to similarity visible in the process. Instead of assessing your inner advisory inner circle, you assess the candidates' characteristics that you have nominated or own, to identify bias for similarity. Often the same kind of similarity dominates in the evaluation of qualifications and performance.

*Such as: succession lists, talent management assessments, interview short lists, leadership recognition programs, hipo talent approved for specialized training courses and events, international mobility, approval for external representation of the company on boards and professional associations, etc.

"FEEL THE NEED" Inclusion Nudge:

IMPLICIT ASSOCIATION TEST INTEGRATED WITH WORK PROCESS

Submitted by: Sharon Kyle, UK D&I Manager, Virgin Media

Why

A cohort of high potential HR professionals were working on a global research project to identify the implications of an ageing population for the company and come up with organisational recommendations from both an employee and customer perspective. Sharon suspected that the HR team's own biases might be creeping into how data and insights were being interpreted during the project – for example, that a youth bias might be skewing how information was being viewed and treated. She wanted to find a way to surface this.

The Inclusion Nudge

Use the Harvard Implicit Association test as an integrated part of qualifying internal research, analysis and recommendations. Use the results of the test taken by the project team members to reflect on biases in analysis and decision-making and to increase objectivity.

How

At a critical stage in the project (when data and insights were being analysed) Sharon invited the team of 20 to complete the Harvard Implicit Associations test on "Young/Old", "Good/Bad" and confidentially send her their results. She collated these and prepared a graph showing the percentage of the team that made various positive associations. The results showed that 95% of the team unconsciously associate young with good (35% strong, 45% moderate, 15% slight, 5% neutral), but none had positive associations between old and good. They began the next project meeting with a facilitated discussion about the implications of these results on their own research and agreed on some ground rules to ensure that age bias was not leading them to interpret information about younger generations more favourably.

Impact

As a result of this practical intervention, the team collectively and individually became more aware of their own biases and were able to mitigate them to present a more balanced project paper and set of proposals to the senior leadership team. As part of the presentation, the team decided to share the experience of uncovering a team bias with the senior leaders, which helped add tangible value to discussions on the topic.

"FEEL THE NEED" Inclusion Nudge:

ILLUSTRATE THE POWER OF IMPLICIT ASSOCIATIONS

Submitted by: Alberto Platz, VP Global Talent & Engagement, D. Swarovski
Corporation AG, ESP

Why

The implicit associations between specific positions and gender are strong but
often invisible, thus difficult to change.

The Inclusion Nudge

Use a simple question *"Can you think of a famous world-class tennis player?"*
The purpose is to get leaders to experience the power of implicit associations
and make them see the results of their answers. Have the leaders make the link
to how this leads to exclusion of a wide range of talents.

How

- Ask colleagues to think of a famous world-class tennis player.
- Have them call out in plenary whom they thought of.
- The experience is that almost all of them will have thought of a male player.
- Then change the question and ask *"Can you think of a female or male world-class tennis player?"*. The experience is that most women and even some men mentioned a woman.

Impact

The impact is a motivated discussion about the quick associations between
jobs/positions and gender.

Authors' Comments

This Inclusion Nudge forces a widening of possibilities to counter stereotyping
and implicit associations. It acts first as a "FEEL THE NEED" Inclusion Nudge and
then becomes a "FRAMING" Inclusion Nudge to help people see the full talent
pool.

"FEEL THE NEED" Inclusion Nudge:

SEE PATTERNS WITH THE D&I LEADERSHIP SHADOW

Submitted by*:* Juliet Bourke, Deloitte
Source of inspiration: Male Champions of Change Leadership Shadow Report
(and tool)[28]

Why

Leaders are likely to be unaware of their image among direct and indirect reports, notably whether the leaders are perceived as authentically committed to Diversity & Inclusion.

The Inclusion Nudge

The "D&I Leadership Shadow" is a tool/intervention where leaders describe and evaluate themselves on how they communicate, demonstrate, signal, and measure their commitment to Inclusion and Diversity, which is compared to how others perceive them and their commitment. This interventions has the purpose of illustrating/showing gaps in self-perception and the perception of others. It is like a mirror, functioning as a push for behavioural change and guiding steps.

How

This tool (see the report) provides a simple way for leaders to examine whether they are influencing I&D as they intend. It is designed to surface inconsistencies between what leaders believe they communicate, demonstrate, prioritise and measure in relation to I&D and what employees hear, observe and understand. Inconsistency creates pressure for alignment.

- **Preparation:** Interview employees about what they "hear" leaders communicate about I&D, what they "see" in their commitment and what they "observe" in how leaders signal their commitment.

- **Leader conversation:** In a one-on-one conversation with a leader, explain that the "D&I Leadership Shadow" is a tool to help leaders see whether the shadow they are casting has the shape, clarity and depth they intend.

- The shadow has four quadrants. Ask the leader to identify in the quadrants how they *communicate* their commitment to inclusion and diversity; *demonstrate* their commitment; *signal* their commitment through the way they allocate their time and resources; and *measure* their impact.

- Starting with the first quadrant, introduce the information gained from interviews conducted with the employees and test for consistency. If none is available, let the leader know that other research shows leaders usually say they communicate their commitment loudly and clearly, but employees usually report hearing silence. *Insight:* This can be because leaders are communicating so many other messages that the D&I one is lost. *Action:* A leader can commit to increasing the level of communication about I&D so that it is as high as other significant business messages – or they can change the way they communicate about I&D.

- Follow the same process for the quadrants on actions, signals, and measures.

Impact

Leaders see their personal "leadership shadow" more clearly and are therefore able to make adjustments to what they say, do, prioritise and measure to ensure their impact is as they intend.

"FEEL THE NEED" Inclusion Nudge:

COMMITMENT TO SELF-DEVELOPMENT AFTER TRAINING

Submitted by: Thais Compoint, Associate Director D&I Europe, Coca Cola Enterprises

Why

It is a challenge for many leaders to translate the insights from unconscious bias training to daily actions and behavioural changes. The purpose of the inclusion nudge is to strengthen business leaders' commitment to their personal action plan following their participation in the "Inclusive Leadership Program", a full-day training on unconscious bias and how to manage differences effectively.

The Inclusion Nudge

Use a structure to publicly share and follow up on commitments coming out of the training course. The Inclusive Leadership Program's participants must share their commitments with their peers out loud. They also have to report to the group, three and six months following the course, what they have done to give life to their commitments.

How

- Ensure that there's time to reflect upon a personal action plan based on the training's key lessons. In our case, to help participants identify *"start, stop, and continue"* areas, they take an inclusive leadership self-assessment at the end of the course.

- Once participants build their action plan, they discuss in trios what they've chosen to do. Trio participants support each other by challenging each other's commitments and sharing good practices.

- After trio discussions, each participant chooses one commitment to share with the entire group. Commitments might relate to any employee life cycle stage.

- At the end of the training, participants identify together the dates for the follow-up meetings, three and six months later.

- The group leader sends everyone an invitation for a conference call during the session. It's important that participants leave the session with the follow-up dates in their diaries.

- Three and six months after the training, participants report on what they've done, the benefits of their actions and challenges they might be facing. They must complete an action plan follow-up template and send it to a corporate e-mail address prior to the meeting.

- During the meetings peers support each other. The meetings are facilitated by the group leader who volunteered to do so during the training.

Impact

Making the commitments public as well as having to report progress to peers makes participants more willing to act upon their personal action plan. They know they'll need to have something to share, and peer pressure increases competition in a positive way.

Authors' Comments

It is a great example of a default nudge when the system is set up to ensure that people don't have to actively opt in, but this is made very easy for them to do. It is also an example of how a simple process of writing down a commitment and say it to a peer (public sharing) can help the brain actually do as intended. One study has shown that by writing down your goals, you were 42% more likely to achieve them. This is similar to the research that illustrated an 18% decrease in patients missing doctor's appointments by simply asking them to write down the appointment details themselves instead of the secretary doing this.

"FEEL THE NEED" Inclusion Nudge:

QUICK INSIGHT IN OUR IMPLICIT ASSOCIATIONS & GENDER / POSITION BIASES

Submitted by: Anita Curle, Global D&I Learning Portfolio Manager, Shell Canada Ltd.

Why

Many people are not aware of how unconscious bias affects their thinking and behaviour. Research from the Harvard Business School (Project Implicit) shows how we have these unreflective associations (both positive and negative) with a variety of characteristics including age, height, accent, skin colour, clothing and weight. And that these are also affecting the perception of competency and related to specific positions and professions.

The Inclusion Nudge

Tell the story/puzzle **Who is the Doctor?** to highlight the impact of implicit associations of gender with professions to raise awareness of gender bias, and to trigger motivation to challenge these kinds of automatic bias.

How

This is a great way to start the conversation with an audience about unconscious bias. It is good to give the audience a visual to focus on for this Inclusion Nudge. It can be done virtually or face-to-face.

> **SAY:** To begin, *"Let's start with a puzzle."*

> **ACTION:** Facilitator walks over to a poster and reads the following story out loud:

> *"A father and his son are driving home from a party. They get into a car accident. The father dies and the son is seriously injured and taken to the hospital. When the doctor comes into the emergency room and looks at the patient, the doctor says, "I can't treat him, he's my son." The question to you is: How is this possible? Who is the doctor?"*

SAY: *"Can you solve this?"* Invite participants to reflect for a minute and then invite responses.

ASK: *"Who is struggling to solve this puzzle?"* Invite their responses first. *"Who thinks they have it solved?"* Invite their responses and discuss.

SAY: *"If your first reaction was "the stepfather" or "the father's father" then you react as most people do: few of us make an automatic association between "doctor" and "female". But actually the doctor in the story is the boy's mother. Despite the fact that we see more and more doctors who are women, such stereotypical associations often control our reactions."*

Researchers note that more than 40% of people on a training course fail to spot the answer. This is an example of our unconscious bias at work, as many of us automatically associate the word "doctor" with the male gender.

Impact

Depending on your audience the reaction can vary. In some countries the puzzle was solved more quickly, and in others it took a long time. When participants (both male and female) hear the answer, they often say, *"of course"*. It makes them realize that they do indeed have gender biases, and that it is natural.

INCLUSION NUDGES

Practical Techniques for Behaviour, Culture, & System Change to Mitigate Unconscious Bias & Create Inclusive Organisations

Authors' Comments

We acknowledge that many I&D practitioners use this story and in various versions. We have decided not to include the names here and only the one who submitted the example.

Suggestion to Strengthen This Powerful Intervention:

When presenting the participants with the research from Project implicit, give them the link to the Implicit Association Test (IAT) and encourage them to take a few tests. It can further the change process if the participants _see_ their biases and become _aware_ of their own automatic associations they should challenge.

You can also ask participants to write down their answer on post-its and then you cluster them on the wall making it very obvious how few had the association doctor/woman.

There are many examples of how simply seeing our own behavioural patterns can change our behaviour. An example is the change of biased NBA referee foul calls[29].

"FEEL THE NEED" Inclusion Nudge:

ILLUSTRATE THE GAP BETWEEN IMPLICIT LEADERSHIP NORMS & NEEDED LEADERSHIP BEHAVIOURS

Submitted by: Janina Norton, Employee Engagement Manager, Company Anonymous[30]

Why

Leadership behaviours/capabilities communicate a clear message about how leaders must behave to succeed. In many companies, visible demonstration of leadership behaviours also contributes to an individual's overall performance rating (therefore having a clear potential influence on career progression). However, they are sometimes developed with the strategic business results in mind (resulting in competition-, success- and power-oriented leadership behaviours such as Results Focus and Commercial Edge). Less consideration is given to the other more people- and culture-oriented styles that are also important for organisational success. Research shows that women and men differ in how they demonstrate different leadership behaviours, but that both styles are necessary for overall organisational success. The challenge for an organisation is to consider whether it's formally communicated leadership behaviours inadvertently set the conditions that make it more likely for one gender to succeed as a leader (and thus progress more easily to more senior leadership positions).

The Inclusion Nudge

Hold an interactive session with leadership to rate leadership behaviours in the organisations and compare to the crucial leadership behaviours identified in research. Identify and illustrate the gender-different ratings and performance scores. Seeing these hidden patterns and gaps are the Inclusion Nudge for more inclusiveness. This intervention interrupts automatic thinking and implicit associations on leadership capabilities and gender.

How

- Present senior leaders with high-level summary of research by McKinsey & Co (2008) identifying the nine organisational behaviours found to improve organisational performance: Participative Decision Making, Role Model, Inspiration, Expectation and Rewards, People Development, Intellectual Stimulation, Efficient Communication, Individualistic Decision Making and Control and Corrective Action.

- Ask leaders to map the organisation's current leadership behaviours to these nine dimensions. For example, Collaboration maps across to Participative Decision Making.

- Then share the next part of the research, which shows that women display the first five leadership behaviours more than men, and men display the last four leadership behaviours more than women. Discuss whether the organisation's leadership behaviours are more weighted towards males or females.

- In organisations that have online performance-management records or otherwise available data, present a summary report showing the average performance of males and females for each leadership behaviour. Often there will be a difference for different behaviours. Also, look at this data within the talent population only.

- Does this align with the research? Does this also demonstrate that it is easier for one gender to be seen as a good leader? Work with the leaders to determine how any inequities can be addressed.

Impact

The process can prompt senior leaders to consider whether the leadership behaviours create the conditions for both males and females to succeed within the organisation, and to make changes as necessary.

 © T. Nielsen & L. Kepinski, 2016
www.inclusion-nudges.org

Authors' Comments

This eye-opener intervention for leaders makes them realise that the implicit leadership norm of the organisation favour men and behaviours more often displayed by men like the research show. It is not sufficient to solely present the rational arguments from research to change the norm. The motivational trigger in this Inclusion Nudge is targeting System 1 thinking ("The Elephant") by engaging the leaders in identifying the hidden patterns and making the gap obvious and visible.

To further leverage the potential in this motivating intervention, it is beneficial to illustrate to the leaders how simple system/process interventions can change this norm, i.e. make the needed leadership behaviours explicit in performance ratings, job adverts, screening criteria etc. Or present some of the "PROCESS" Inclusion Nudges in this Guidebook.

To promote change motivation is important address System 1 thinking and equally important to shrink complexity and script some easy and critical first steps (which taps into System 2 thinking).

"FEEL THE NEED" Inclusion Nudge:

SHOW HIDDEN PATTERNS IN PERFORMANCE CALIBRATION DATA

Submitted by: Gudrun Sander, Director for Diversity and Management Programs, University of St. Gallen

Why

To overcome a tendency toward overconfidence in data and a strong belief in performance evaluations as objective, fair and a true picture of reality. The challenge is to question if performance evaluations are reliable enough to serve as a basis for promotion decisions.

The Inclusion Nudge

Identify and show to leaders the patterns in performance ratings that the data is not showing, for example correlations between a supervisor's gender or age and the gender and age of the employees and their ratings.

In the organisation where this intervention was done, it worked as a "FEEL THE NEED" Inclusion Nudge because there was a very clear pattern that surprised them:

- Male supervisors rated their male employees higher than female employees.
- Female supervisors also rated male employees higher than female employees.
- When the supervisor was older than the employee: the larger the age difference, the better the performance rating.
- When the supervisor was younger than the employee: the larger the age difference, the worse the performance rating.

How

- Analyse the data from the performance and potential ratings and identify hidden patterns/correlations of the supervisor's gender/age/nationality etc. and the ratings of the employees and the same characteristics. Also look for other potential biases like height, educational background etc.

© T. Nielsen & L. Kepinski, 2016
www.inclusion-nudges.org

- Show / illustrate (with graphs, pictures, images, colours) the patterns / correlation to the top management team and the diversity and inclusion council.

Facilitate a discussion about possible reasons for this and inform them about biases and implicit associations (positive and negative).

Impact

Due to this Inclusion Nudge, the motivation to change was created. Each leader wanted to know how this looked in his or her unit. The dialogue became much more engaged. They discussed honest reasons for this result. They realised these performance evaluations were not as reliable as they thought and perhaps not enough basis for promotions. The next step is to present to the line managers, who need to take action on this issue and be accountable for progress.

Authors' Comments

This Inclusion Nudge is a great example of how simple the intervention is, but how deep an analytical dive you have to make in the data to identify the root cause of inequality and get the data to design the Inclusion Nudge. You could potentially leverage more of the potential in this Inclusion Nudge, by engaging the leaders in identifying other areas in talent decisions and business decisions where biases could potentially play out. Also ask them how they will proactively make sure to mitigate the impact of biases in the future (make sure you have some suggestions).

This "FEEL THE NEED" Inclusion Nudge could also be used as an integrated part of the performance calibration process. The more recent the bias awareness/eye-opener is, the less bias seem to interfere in performance ratings.

"FEEL THE NEED" Inclusion Nudge:

"WALK THE LINE" TO ENGAGE IN SPONSORSHIP PROGRAMS

Submitted by: Sarah Boddey, EMEA D&I Manager, AIG

Why

Getting participants in career development programs to understand the power of a sponsor.

The Inclusion Nudge

An interactive exercise with the purpose of helping senior leaders (gender mixed group) identify and see the hidden patterns and links between number of promotions and number of sponsors. The exercise is to have leaders line up on a physical line that illustrate a scale from few to many promotions and have them show on a note with the number of sponsors (formal and informal) they have had in their career). Often this number correlate with where on the line they stand. This Inclusion Nudge illustrates how sponsorship result in more promotions and that women often have fewer sponsors and promotions.

How

Use the exercise when running a leadership session on talent development and the importance of having a sponsor.

- Ask all the career development program attendees to write down the number of sponsors (formal or informal) they've had during their career. Ask them to fold their piece of paper in half so no one else can see it.

- Then ask them to make a silent mental note of the number of promotions they've had over their career. Give them a couple of minutes to calculate.

- Have all attendees stand up and move to one side of the room. Ask them to arrange themselves in one long line, with the person who's had the most number of promotions at one end, going down to the least at the other end.

- Once they are in line, ask them then to unfold and hold up their piece of paper. They will then naturally look at each other's answers.

- What usually happens is:
    - The line goes from being more male-dominated at one end (more promotions) to being more female dominated at the other end (fewer promotions).

    - The people at the end of the line with the higher number of promotions usually are also holding up numbers that show a higher number of sponsors.

Impact

Participants have a very visual and tangible way of seeing how people with sponsors have usually been promoted more often than those without them. This makes senior leaders more supportive of sponsorship programs and more engaged in these kinds of organisations initiatives (instead of leaving it up to the individual).

Authors' Comments:

Often organisations use mentoring programs as a "solution" for increasing women at senior leadership levels. However, mentoring is a career development tool, and one that is disproportionately applied to women than men in organisations. It is often said that women are "over-mentored". And typically the results of promotion of mentees tends to be nil to low. To truly impact women's advancement to senior positions, many organisations are turning towards Sponsorship programs. These are aimed at connecting the sponsoree to senior level executives. Thus, building influential relationships and opening visibility to the full talent pipeline in order to make equable, fully informed decisions on promotion and succession planning.

It can be a challenge to first launch a Sponsorship program, despite the wealth of research and case studies on the value of Sponsorship (which appeals to System 2 "rational" thinking). Usually it's an emotional unconscious reaction (System 1 thinking) against these new programs, as it entails recognition that senior leaders don't have the same type of relationships with all in the talent pipeline and/or don't know well the hipo talents, etc. The foundational concept of Sponsorship is grounded upon often unexamined areas of one's informal networks, and "in groups" and "out groups" dynamics. Often there is a reaction from seniors leaders of, *"I don't do anything special for men (or the majority population), why should I do anything different for women (or the minority population)?"* This can become a significant blocker to the success of Sponsorship programs and must be addressed. A "FEEL THE NEED" Inclusion Nudge, such as this one, is ideal for this situation.

"FEEL THE NEED" Inclusion Nudge:

SHARING PERSONAL STORIES TO BUILD TRUST

Submitted by: Julie O'Mara, O'Mara and Associates

Why

Leaders and D&I professionals may find it difficult to 1) get a message across to others, 2) build trust and 3) relate to those who are different from themselves. It can be difficult for the 'members' of the majority or the privileged to see the advantages they have and disadvantages others have – often there is a blindness towards gender, race, ethnicity etc.

The Inclusion Nudge

Telling personal stories about inclusion and exclusion. Use stories that are genuine, meaningful, crisp, and relevant to an issue, as they can be powerful tools for bridging differences and making people feel the implications of our behaviour.

How

Stories can create images in the mind of participants/the listener and trigger feelings of inclusion and exclusion without having experienced this themselves. A powerful story is relatable, humble, true, believable, told in a context that others can understand and perhaps identify with, and relevant to the learning point.

- Think of situations you have faced that relate to D&I, such as when you felt stereotyped, when you realized you were biased, when you said something you should not have, when you felt the help of an ally and so forth.

- Write down your stories – try for a dozen or so as you will need several for different purposes and audiences. Hone the stories.

- Practice your delivery in front of a mirror.

- Deliver your stories to a knowledgeable colleague. Hone your story again. Practice, practice, practice.

- And don't overuse a story - have a repertoire.

Impact

The impact can be immediate for understanding the learning point, but it doesn't stop there. The leader or D&I professional (the story teller) become someone whom others begin to see as relatable and as a colleague/ally in achieving what matters in D&I work.

"FEEL THE NEED" Inclusion Nudge:

HOW IT FEELS TO BE EXCLUDED

Submitted by: Eric Dziedzic, CEO, CRxSolutions

Why

Changing exclusive behaviour is difficult because most people can't see the impact of their behaviours.

The Inclusion Nudge

Illustrate the impact of certain non-inclusive behaviours and provide a transparent forum for discussion about how employees feel about exclusion, from the perspective of those who are excluded.

How

Create a scenario in which two candidates of similar but not equal qualifications are interviewing for one open position that illustrates a typical experience (for example, the hiring manager finds the slightly less qualified candidate more appealing based on network familiarity or similar experiences, such as attending the same university). Emphasise familiar barriers: older vs. younger worker; men vs. women, college graduates vs. work experience) and unfold with a predictable result.

End the scenario with a series of questions regarding the hiring manager's rationale. The point is to elicit emotional responses to the scenarios – there are no wrong answers.

Demonstrate the scenario at manager's meetings or during training programs. Have a skilled facilitator lead the discussion.

Impact

Leaders are motivated to reflect on their own exclusive behaviour and to challenge it.

"FEEL THE NEED" Inclusion Nudge

SECTION SUMMARY

Keep in mind that the purpose of "FEEL THE NEED" Inclusion Nudges are to target the unconscious system of the brain (1) that is emotionally driven in order to create an emotional trigger that motivates to behavioural change. These behavioural interventions also promote a more reflective process in System 2 of the potential implications of the status quo behaviour. These kinds of Inclusion Nudges often need the other two types of Inclusion Nudges to support the actual change or the kind of interventions that the Heath Brothers suggest in their book SWITCH on how to steer the elephant's rider (System 2) in the right direction.

See Section 7 for information on designing "FEEL THE NEED" Inclusion Nudges.

© T. Nielsen & L. Kepinski, 2016
www.inclusion-nudges.org

Section 4: EXAMPLES OF "PROCESS" INCLUSION NUDGES

Reminder:

"PROCESS" Inclusion Nudges are intended to help people *make better decisions and leverage diversity*. This is done by altering elements of such organisational processes as candidate screening, promotions, performance reviews and successor planning. It also involves collaborative processes like meetings and facilitation.

© T. Nielsen & L. Kepinski, 2016
www.inclusion-nudges.org

Inspirational Thoughts

"You are wise to be targeting the Elephant (unconscious system of the brain) when it comes to diversity; so much of the training I've seen is Rider-focused (rational system of the brain), to its detriment." **– Dan Heath** *(e-mail response to Tinna and Lisa on Inclusion Nudges info)*

"...a brief glimpse at human fallibility. The picture that emerges is one of busy people trying to cope in a complex world in which they cannot afford to think deeply about every choice they have to make." **– Thaler and Sunstein**

"Tweaking the environment is about making the right behaviours a little bit easier and the wrong behaviours a little bit harder. It's that simple." **– Chip and Dan Heath**

"Probably the most important way that bias affects organisations is in the way we manage talent. ... Remember that in any aspect of the talent management process there are biases on both sides: the rater biases of the people who are doing the evaluating or hiring, and the self-rater bias of the person who is being evaluated." **– Howard Ross**

© T. Nielsen & L. Kepinski, 2016
www.inclusion-nudges.org

Inspirational Thoughts *Continued*

"Organisations are created by us and so inevitably bias will be built into every aspect unless we remain very aware and vigilant. ... Discrimination seeps into organisational practices....[which can] dictate the core of the individual's experience. It's what the organisation does that creates its effect on us, not what it says about what it does. Processes, functions and standards are constantly questioned in today's business environments as organisations look to improve efficiency and quality We must also challenge our official and unofficial practices to make sure they embody the diversity goals we have set for the organisation." – **Binna Kandola**

"PROCESS" Inclusion Nudge:

JOINT INSTEAD OF INDIVIDUAL EVALUATION FOR PERFORMANCE TO TRIUMPH GENDER BIAS

Submitted by: Prof. Dr. Iris Bohnet, Women and Public Policy Program, Harvard's Kennedy School

Why

Gender-blind evaluations are virtually impossible. It is often not possible to evaluate candidates behind a screen, as many major symphony orchestras do in their auditions of new musicians. As *"seeing is believing"* and we tend not to see many male kindergarten teachers and female CEOs, evaluators will be more likely to favour women for jobs as kindergarten teachers and men as CEOs. Inside our organisations we see the same associations between a specific gender and specific positions, functions, and roles when these traditionally have been and still are dominated by one gender.

The Inclusion Nudge

Make joint evaluations of candidates a part of the recruitment / promotion/performance calibration process instead of the typical individual evaluations.

To overcome gender bias in the evaluation of job candidates, we change procedures to make it easy for our biased minds to get it right and hire/promote the most qualified rather than the ones with demographic similarities with the norm. Joint evaluation, in contrast to separate evaluation, replaces our internal (automatic and associative) referent, the "norm", with an actual referent, building on the insight in Prospect Theory that there are no absolute but only relative judgments. This evaluation nudge affects whom candidates are compared with, thus how competent they are perceived and who is selected.

How

Evaluate candidates comparatively – which is more likely to be done in hiring than in promotion or job assignment decisions, and also at junior rather than senior levels.

© T. Nielsen & L. Kepinski, 2016
www.inclusion-nudges.org

Standard promotion decisions

- Require supervisors to recommend at least two people for consideration for promotion to force them to evaluate their pool comparatively.

- Have a promotion committee evaluate all suggested candidates comparatively, focusing on performance criteria that are as objective as possible. Be aware that gender bias tends to be particularly pronounced not when evaluating people based on past performance but rather when judging future potential.

One-off promotion decisions, for example to counter an outside offer

If you do not have the luxury of evaluating various candidates simultaneously but have to respond to market pressures, trigger different referents in the evaluators' minds by sharing a sample of people who have recently been promoted to the level under consideration. Include counter-stereotypical examples to avoid automatic comparisons with the "ideal" or "typical" person (biased implicit norm).

Impact

People conducting joint evaluations are much more likely to choose job candidates based on their past performance and not their gender bias. In separate evaluations they are more likely to choose job candidates based on their gender. See research listed at the end of the Guidebook: *When Performance Trumps Gender Bias: Joint Versus Separate Evaluation.*

"PROCESS" INCLUSION NUDGE:
GROUP INTERVIEWS

Submitted by: Stephen Frost, CEO of Frost Included, former Head of Diversity & Inclusion at The London Organising Committee of the Olympic and Paralympic Games (LOCOG)

Why

When people interview one-to-one, they think they are being objective in the interview situation, evaluation, and selection, but they are unfortunately biased. At the London Organising Committee of the Olympic Games 2012 (LOCOG) two interventions were implemented to reduce bias. One was to have interview panels of a minimum of three people, in order to have as many diverse perspectives and behaviours available. The other intervention was the one described below as a "PROCESS" Inclusion Nudge.

The Inclusion Nudge

Interview candidates in groups of 5-8 (if not a bundle then always interview more than one candidate).

As the research by Iris Bohnet et al. has identified, this reduces stereotypes and bias, and forces the unconscious mind to focus on performance. Also, we tend to select more variety in bundles. When people are evaluated in groups relatively to each other their individual characteristics (e.g. gender) are less salient and their skill sets and how they interact with the group are more evident. In group interviews, the interviewers can see skills and attributes play out in real time.

How

- Make sure to have a strategic workforce plan so you know what talent you actually want and what gaps currently exist in your toolbox.
- Identify based on the plan the positions you need people for and what you need (hiring criteria). Use this intervention of group interview with more generic positions and when you are hiring for multiple

openings/positions of the same kind of role e.g. 5 programme managers (not specialists).

- For positions where you need to hire 5, shortlist 15, and interview in 3 groups of 5 and choose 2 candidates per group, or interview 8 and choose 4 candidates. The larger the group, the more powerful the diversity nudge.
- The interview panel should have a mix of gender and functions
- Give the candidates an exercise/task to solve that is related to the job for which you are hiring. The candidates are solving the task in the room as a group. There are no specific framing instructions other than solve the task to the best of your ability.
- The interview panel evaluates the candidate, such as in an assessment centre, by observing their behaviour and skills accordingly to the predetermined qualification criteria. Group of candidates all together, each person assessed individually as part of the group exercise.
- Do two rounds of interview. In the 1st interview the hiring manager participates as part of the interview panel, in the 2nd interview the hiring manager is not participating (to reduce potential for bias).
- Each interviewer scores the candidates on screening criteria independently. The interview panel compares scores only afterwards.

Impact

The Olympic Games in London 2012 had the most diverse workforce in history. Other inclusive practices were implemented in addition to the Group Interviews. The numbers speaks for itself but so do the stories.

- Workforce composition:
    - Race: 60% white/40% black, Asian, or minority ethnic
    - Gender/gender identity: 54% male/46% female (trans staff included)
    - Disability: 9% (deaf, disabled or having a long-term health condition)
    - Sexual orientation: 5% declared lesbian, gay or bisexual
    - Age: 36% under 30, 15% over 50 with ranges from 16-79
    - Faith: All major faiths represented
    - Economic Inclusion / Social Mobility: 36% of hired people were previously unemployed and 23% came from the poorest boroughs in East London.

- A straight, white male venue manager shared his experience with Stephen, that he *would never have met people like that* in his previous or next intended professional setting. He wouldn't have talked to *them* in the street or a bar, let alone work with them. They weren't *his kind of people* but they became his beloved team.
- Furthermore, group interviews reduce cost and save time Also in the situation of pressure to reduce the time to hire, this is a positive impact on what is usually is an anti-diversity process.

Authors' Comments

Also refer to Iris Bohnet's "PROCESS" Inclusion Nudge entitled 'JOINT INSTEAD OF INDIVIDUAL EVALUATION FOR PERFORMANCE TO TRIUMPH GENDER BIAS'.

We see more and more organisations using this process as part of their evaluation and selection process for their graduate and talent programmes. Additional to group interviews, candidates make group assignments and presentations.

We highly recommend reading Stephen Frost's inspirational book *The Inclusion Imperative: How Real Inclusion Creates Better Business and Builds Better Societies*. Not only do you get concrete tested and proven tools to implement, but you also read the personal stories from the journey of the diverse Olympic and Paralympic Games of London in 2012.

"PROCESS" Inclusion Nudge:

"INTERRUPTER" TO PROMOTE OBJECTIVITY IN TALENT DEVELOPMENT DISCUSSIONS

Submitted by: Axel Jentzsch, BASF SE, Diversity + Inclusion

Why

In talent development meetings, discussions often lack objectivity and unconscious biases can be difficult to address. Looking for data and facts that confirm existing impressions leads to increased sharing of rumours, gossip and judgments instead of real observations.

The Inclusion Nudge

Use a bell as a tool as an 'interrupter' to make 'an auditory attention impact' in talent development/performance review processes in order address and mitigate bias in the discussions, thus increase objectivity and shift the mode of thinking of the evaluators from 'associative' to 'reflective'.

How

During talent development discussions, all managers were given a hotel-reception bell to put in front of them. They were instructed to make immediate use of this bell whenever they experienced – or suspected – that someone was sharing an assumption, bias, stereotype, rumour or gossip rather than a real personal experience or facts about performance, or whenever the experience was presented not as a neutral observation but as a judgment.

Impact

This Inclusion Nudge helped managers understand how often and how quickly talent development discussions deviated from the objective exchange of observations and allowed them to quickly get back "on track".

"PROCESS" Inclusion Nudge:

GENDER BALANCED CANDIDATE GROUPS IN TRAINEE ASSESSMENTS

Submitted by: Anonymous

Why

Female candidates tended to hold back their participation during assessments because the group of aspirants was male-dominated. We wanted to get a balanced contribution of male and female candidates as part of the recruiting process for the trainee program.

The Inclusion Nudge

Create gender-balanced groups of candidates to increase participation by women, resulting in more equal assessments of female and male candidates.

How

One of the organisation's programs for recent graduates consisted of a two-year trainee program in which trainees were given real jobs while they went through two different assignments in functional areas. During assessments, the gender composition of the aspirant group used to be dominated by men who participated vocally while female aspirants held back their comments. For this reason, it was proposed to change the composition of the groups to 50% female and 50% male. With gender-balanced groups a better performance of female candidates was achieved. Female candidates became more involved in the proposed activities with a greater likelihood of being chosen.

Impact

The result was greater participation of female candidates during assessments and better performance of the entire group, providing women with a better chance of keeping up in the process to become a trainee.

Authors' Comments

This Inclusion Nudge has the purpose of influencing the behaviour of the candidates not the evaluators. By simply changing the composition of the candidate groups that are being assessed it is possible to make the process more inclusive and opportunities for engagement more equal.

The same intervention can be used to mitigate national/cultural differences in these kind of assessment groups, but in some cases we might need to create homogeneous groups instead. Often nationality/ethnic differences in how to engage in groups impact the assessment of candidates' performance. Some organisations (with Western dominant organisational culture) experience that Asians do not lean in and claim their space as much as "Western" candidates in group assessments. Often this has a negative impact on the performance evaluation of Asian candidates. If we tap into the knowledge from research on social change, we need to create a "Free space" of similarity (an Asian group) to reduce our internal referent, the "Western norm" (Prospect Theory), and to avoid the dominance of the majority group behaviour (get inspiration from K. Kellogg's research in the resource list).

"PROCESS" Inclusion Nudge:

WORK FLEXIBILITY & 80% POSITIONS AS THE NORM

The authors have merged several submissions due to similarities in approach and impact.

Submitted by: Nia Joynson-Romanzina, Global Head of Diversity & Inclusion, UBS; Ursula A. Wynhoven, General Counsel, United Nations Global Compact (source of inspiration: Telsta, AU); Alison Maitland, author[31] and consultant; Veronika Hucke, D&I Strategy & Solutions

Why

Flexible working is still seen by many organisations as the exception to the norm and as a benefit or arrangement for certain categories of employee, notably women with children. As a result, line managers often regard it as a cost and burden, while many employees, especially men, fear that asking for it will be career limiting. Furthermore, all too frequently, hiring managers believe that a job can be carried out successfully only by a full-time employee, possibly due to following traditional working models. Many candidates (especially women, but increasingly men) are not interested or able to work according to these traditional norms, and therefore will not apply or be encouraged to apply. Nonetheless, when asked, managers usually want to have roles filled full-time and tend to exclude part-time candidates from the short list. These implicit norms limit an organisation's ability to hire/promote the best qualified people, and to increase the share of applicants and hires of diverse backgrounds and preferences. Those who choose or need to work "differently" may be seen as lacking commitment because they do not fit the ideal of the always-available worker.

The Inclusion Nudge

Position work flexibility as the norm from the beginning.

Flip the implicit norm of the 'ideal way of working' by flipping the default of all positions having to be worked full time, and in a specific location making it easier for all employees to work in flexible/agile arrangements. Change the default in the system to 80-90% positions and in agile working arrangements. Make managers argue why flexible work arrangements (the norm) are not possible in a particular position (opt out) instead of arguing why one candidate should have 'special treatment' (opt in). This can be done systemically in job descriptions and advertisements.

How

- Change the choice process of the hiring manager by change the design of the organisations process and standard. This has to start with the job description.
  - o Instead of thinking of work as a place, think of it as a series of activities. Only restrict where and when these activities are done if there are logical constraints about time and place – obvious examples are retail sales assistants in a store or autoworkers on an assembly line.
  - o Consider what kinds of support and technology people need to do some or all of their activities remotely (e.g. from a home office or a smart work hub near their home).

- Tell managers that all jobs can be worked on an agile/flexible schedule or as an 80-90% position unless proven otherwise. Use the "opt-out" approach, change the thinking from "*Can this job be done through agile working?*" to "*Why would this job not be suitable for agile working?*"
  - o Question thinking that is not open to agile working, asking "*Is this is the most productive approach?*"
  - o Cite the body of research showing that people are generally more productive when they have greater control over where and when they carry out their tasks (see the book *Future Work*).
  - o Ask "*Why is someone who works long hours in the office seen as more dedicated than a colleague who completes work quickly and leaves promptly, or who works a day or two from home each week? Which of them is more productive, focused, and loyal? Why does it matter where someone is, as long as they are responsive, meet clients' needs and achieve their agreed goals?*"

- Advertise jobs at all levels with flexibility clearly built in. [32]

- Post all roles as 80% positions and suppress information on preferred work time and location of candidates in early selection stages.
- Ensure that the hiring manager is aware of the candidate's work time/location preferences at the interview. This avoids awkward situations and ensures that both parties know what to expect if i.e. a part-time candidate is selected.
- Seek out senior people in your organisation who are doing their jobs in an agile or flexible way and encourage them to share their stories. Talk about them when recruiting or promoting others.

Impact

- A broader and more diverse group of applicants
- Gender-balanced project teams
- A noticeable increase in the number of applications from women
- Qualitative evidence that hiring managers are more willing to accept reduced work time if they have a preference for a specific candidate.
- Make it easier to attract international candidates, that might not be internationally mobile for relocation but for commuting.

Here are two Impact examples from Allison Maitland's book *Future Work*:

- The first comes from Niall FitzGerald, co-chairman of Unilever when Alison interviewed him for the Financial Times in 2003. Aiming for more gender-balanced senior leadership, he explained how the Executive Committee had needed to change their thinking about flexibility. *"There was lots of enthusiasm and one colleague said: 'We must identify very clearly those jobs which can be operated in a flexible manner'. My response was: 'You're going in absolutely the wrong direction. We will say: 'In principle every job can be operated in a flexible manner unless it can be demonstrably shown to be otherwise.' That immediately changed the mindset."* In the last few years, Unilever has become a global leader in agile working.

- The second example comes from Mike Dean, managing director of Accenture's business process outsourcing business in the UK, Ireland and the Nordics. A mobile worker himself without a fixed office, Dean works to change attitudes about how and where jobs are done. *"There are still pockets where managers think that everyone has to be in the office seven days a week,"* he says. *"We have to change these attitudes. Someone will say to me, 'This role has to be five days a week, and it has to be London-based,' and I'll look at it and say, 'I don't think it needs to be done that way.'"* (See case study in Chapter 5 of *Future Work*.)

Authors' Comments

This Inclusion Nudges is also a "FRAMING" Inclusion Nudge because it reframes the connotations to 'flexible' work as 'part time work for women'. By applying the word 'agile' instead of 'flexible' it might be possible to change the anchor of the thought process from a perception of flexible work arrangement being a women issue to being an organisational development issue (future proofing the organisation through agility).

This could also help change another dominant connotation to *part-time jobs* = *"only part-time engaged"'*. This is often a bias experienced by people in part-time positions (both men and women). This can potentially limit their career opportunities, and limit the organisation's utility of their potential.

"PROCESS" Inclusion Nudge:

BLIND SCREENING IN RECRUITMENT PROCESS

Submitted by: Sarah Margles, D&I specialist Public Service of Toronto, CA, and Tinna C. Nielsen, Founder of Move the Elephant for Inclusiveness.[33]

Why

Often the screening/evaluation process for a new hire or promotion is influenced by such visual impressions as the layout and style of a resume or application, as well as by implicit associations to gender, skin colour, age and other biases. This is also the case in the analysis of test results, in interviews and in the selection processes. To ensure a fair process and selection of the best candidates, it is crucial to design the process to be as objective as possible. Unconscious bias awareness and intercultural intelligence are not enough to make the screening and selection process objective. It is necessary to implement steps that help the brain make better decisions and reduce the negative impact of biases – challenging the behavioural drivers of "status quo", "mindless choice" and "confirmation bias".

The Inclusion Nudge

Make candidates anonymous in the evaluation and selection process by removing as much identity data as possible.

How

There are different opportunities to integrate this intervention as part of existing organisational process and systems:

- In the e-recruiting system demographic identity factors such as gender, age, name and photo are not revealed to the recruiting panel during the first screening process. Only when the candidates for interviewing have been selected is identity information given to the recruiting panel.

- When resumes come in, have an assistant manually remove names and geographic information, assigning each resume a number. When possible, ask applicants to submit their resume using a template you have designed, so that layout is consistent.

- Provide screening tests electronically, and have all submissions formatted with consistent styling, again with names removed and replaced with a number.

- Require that search agencies deliver candidates on long/short list anonymously. Require information about the search agency's screening criteria for the long list. Always require diverse candidates, gender as a minimum.

- Have one member of the recruiting team interview candidates by phone. Experience show that this person will often have a different perspective on the candidate because the evaluation is not being "distracted" by looks and gestures.

Impact

More diversity in the final pool due to a more objective process, thus a better chance of selecting the best qualified candidate and promoting equal opportunity and diversity.

Authors' Comments

Here is an example of how this Inclusion Nudge has been applied within another organisation:

In 2014, Tinna C. Nielsen led a session for IBM Denmark's top leadership team with 'Feel the Need' Inclusion Nudges (from the guidebook) designed as exercises and eye-openers illustrating the gaps between their self-perception/good intentions and their actual (biased) behaviour. It was decided to build an internal community of champions to master and spread the techniques in IBM Denmark. The (former) CEO was to select a diverse group of 12 leaders in the organisation based on their application. Ulla Dalsgaard (one of IBM Denmark's Diversity Leads) gave him a list of 50 anonymous applicants. The CEO said: " How am I supposed to choose when I cannot see who they are?" As soon as he had said that he realised that this was exactly why he needed help with selecting the team objectively, and not in a biased manner. She had helped him 'Feel the Need' with a 'Process' Inclusion Nudge of anonymising the applicants.

What Ulla had done was to apply the 'Blind Screening' Inclusion Nudge to help them to choose objectively from the list of candidates. Awareness about bias and the motivation created by the 'FEEL THE NEED' Inclusion Nudges from the leadership sessions was not enough to create a non-biased selection. With this 'PROCESS' Inclusion Nudge of anonymising the applicants Ulla had made sure the selection would be objective according to the qualification criteria.

Tinna facilitated a full learning lab process for the community in 2015. They used some of the 'FEEL THE NEED' Inclusion Nudges to get buy-in from the new CEO. The community has now been assigned several corporate tasks by the executive team and other teams in the organisation are asking for their assistance.

"PROCESS" Inclusion Nudge:

NEUTRAL OBSERVER IN TALENT DISCUSSIONS

Submitted by: Charlotte Sweeney, Charlotte Sweeney Associates

Why

Although unconscious bias awareness training had been rolled out in the organisation, there was concern about how this translated into reduction of bias in talent discussions.

The Inclusion Nudge

Use "neutral" observation and feedback from observer (plus video recording) as an integrated part of the talent review process to reduce bias in the evaluation and selection process.

How

As they approached the annual promotions period, I asked two senior leaders if they would be interested in their promotions team taking part in an experiment. The aim was to observe how people behaved in a group decision-making process and if their biases influenced decision-making. Both leaders agreed; they were interested to see the outcome.

During the experiment,

- I gained agreement from all participants to video record the meeting in which they made the final decisions as to who would gain a promotion that year and who would be considered the following year.

- At the beginning of the meeting I asked all attendees to have their discussion as if they weren't being recorded. I said I would purely observe throughout and that I would ask questions after the process had finished, and then we would review some of the footage. The meeting started, and after a few minutes all attendees felt comfortable and had forgotten about the recording.

- Once the decisions on promotions had been made, I asked the attendees to reflect on how easy it was to come to a consensus about who would be promoted and if they felt they had been fair and equitable throughout the process.

    o All felt they had given the candidates a fair review and that the right people were going to get promoted.

- I then asked them to consider the words and phrases they used for the different candidates as they discussed them and if they felt that any bias had slipped into their discussions.

    o None of the attendees could recall any examples where they had spoken about the promotions differently.

- I shared a couple of examples, including:

    o *"You referred to one male as committed to his role, not ready for the promotion yet but at risk of leaving if you didn't promote him this year. You also spoke about a female candidate who you thought was 90% ready this year but that an extra year would make sure she was REALLY ready. What was the difference between those two decisions?"*

    o *"You referred to one person who was excelling at their job and had outstanding performance ratings for the last four years; however, you didn't know if you should promote this person because the new manager in that area has a 'thing' about people without a degree. How did that shape your thinking?"*

    o There were a number of other examples I shared to gain their views on their decision-making process.
    o Many couldn't recall those specific aspects of the discussions and were not sure they had actually been said.

- At that stage I replayed elements of the recording for all in the room to hear the discussions and to also watch their body language on the screen. We continued a discussion about what was happening

 © T. Nielsen & L. Kepinski, 2016
www.inclusion-nudges.org

throughout the meeting after they had watched some of the footage. Although this process did take some time to complete, it was clear that many in the room had not consciously been aware of some of the comments or body language until they watched the video.

Impact

After watching the playback of the video, they felt they needed to review some of the decisions and discuss again. Different decisions were made in a few cases. Feedback from the attendees was hugely positive; they felt more aware of the impact unconscious bias had on their everyday decision-making. As a result of the experiment, the process of recording the discussions and reviewing the videos as a decision-making team was introduced throughout the promotions process for a specific region and recommended for delivery in other regions.

Authors' Comments

This process is terrific if you can get an organisation to agree to have their talent management discussions videotaped. This helps to address first a "FEEL THE NEED" Inclusion Nudge with holding a mirror to the leader's own spoken and non-verbal communications regarding talent to reflect what upon what is unreflected. The video becomes the "FEEL THE NEED" Inclusion Nudge to shift awareness and attention. Seeing is believing. Then the focus on how talent is discussed becomes the supporting "PROCESS" Inclusion Nudge to support the previous nudge.

To take this a step further, and one that can be self-managed by the team, see the "PROCESS" Inclusion Nudge entitled 'Interrupters to Promote Objectivity in Talent Development Discussions', submitted by: Axel Jentzsch, BASF SE, Diversity + Inclusion.

"PROCESS" Inclusion Nudge:

SHIFT THE THINKING IN THE PERFORMANCE CALIBRATION PROCESS

Submitted by: Anita Cassagne, People Development Manager & Gender Balance Lead, Nestlé Waters, and Sue Johnson, Global D&I Leader, Nestlé

Why

While the common perception is that women advance up the corporate ladder until they reach a "glass ceiling", the reality is different. Women actually drop off at almost every grade level. Changing this requires understanding what is going on. Mostly, it is due to unconscious biases from both women and men, as well as the corporate cultures that influence what talent is perceived like. This unconscious bias and organisational norm have a strong impact on people's perceptions. Eliminating stereotypes requires effort on the part of both men and women, as well as the organisation. People may automatically and unconsciously use stereotypes to arrive at judgments. Attention will be paid to different kinds of information depending on whether the employee is female or male. Hence, different performance standards may unintentionally be applied to women and men.

The Inclusion Nudge

An 'enabler' brochure with a pair of paper "glasses" as a prompter to *"Put your gender glasses on...to assess talent"* as part of the people calibration process. The material is on the table during a talent discussion and used to qualify the evaluation process. The purpose is to get participants to shift their mode of thinking from the unconscious system to the reflected system in the brain.

How

- Design the material/brochure with information and enablers on how to mitigate bias and with the paper glasses.
- When all candidates have been discussed, dedicate part of the discussion to women in the talent pipeline. Ask the leaders as part of this process step to read the brochure and put on the 'gender glasses'. Talk about performance, potential, competencies and skills, using supporting evidence to illustrate situations to make sure all potential gender biases are eliminated.
- Instruct participants to not talk about the employee's personal situation.
- If high-potential women are removed from the list, the manager should account for the removal. Challenge assumptions.
- Implement supporting actions: 1) Develop clear career development plans for all high-potential women and follow up its implementation. Support their development and track their career and progress. 2) Review job assignments of top talents on an annual basis to ensure they are working on projects with high visibility, developmental opportunities and impact.

Impact

- Force a shift in the mode of thinking in the evaluation process/situation.
- More qualified and gender neutral performance discussions.

Authors' Comments

The "gender glasses" became a physical symbol for a shift in the process...to reflect on how the previous talent discussion went relative to the stated intentions of working towards gender balance. Symbols are often more powerful than words, and deeply embedded in the subconscious and processed rapidly. The "glasses" triggered the needed action for "looking", or in this case by putting on the glasses after the first round of talent discussions, triggered to "re-look" (review) the discussion and the results.

We recommend to combine many of the Inclusion Nudges. This Inclusion Nudge could be combined with the Inclusion Nudge on changing the default from 'Who is ready for a successor plan?' and 'Why?' to 'All are ready now.' and 'Why not?'.

"PROCESS" Inclusion Nudge:

REDUCE CONFORMITY & LEVERAGE DIVERSITY OF THOUGHT IN GROUPS

Submitted by: Tinna C. Nielsen, Founder of Move the Elephant for Inclusiveness

Why

Implicit norms for the right way to perform, information bias, and group dynamics like socialisation, conformity and groupthink are barriers to leveraging diversity of thought and creating a truly inclusive culture. Often managers, facilitators and project leaders encourage team members to share their points of view and perspectives, or raise their critical voices. The intentions are good, but research like Solomon Asch's experiments on conformity show that group dynamics are a powerful force that makes individuals conform to the opinion of the majority. We do not want to rock the boat, we are afraid of being perceived as incompetent or we believe that what the majority of peers think must be right. As social beings we have a basic need to feel accepted by the group. We conform unconsciously – and sometimes consciously. Recent research also shows that even when women in leadership groups are encouraged to share their perspectives they do so less often than men. Asch's research also shows that people conform less to the group norm when they are asked to write their perspectives or share them with one peer (an ally). Asch concludes that this is due to having less at stake. To leverage more of the full potential of each individual, processes are needed to reduce the negative impact of group dynamics.

The Inclusion Nudge

Instead of asking people in a group to speak up or share their perspective verbally, make it an integrated part of the work process (meeting, training, decision-making, discussion, talent review etc.) to leverage diverse perspectives with simple interventions, such as write on paper/post-it or share perspectives in pairs and then tell each other's perspectives to the larger group. The interventions are designed for the process to be inclusive as well as psychologically safe, and all team members are being 'pushed' in a non-intrusive way to participate.

How

Below is a description on how to implement these non-intrusive interventions in an organisation and the ways of working. At Arla leaders are introduced to this way of working through the leadership program and a two-day team sessions on inclusive leadership and team development. The leaders then use the same simple process and Inclusion Nudges in their own daily leadership and in the way they involve/engage their teams in new ways of collaborating and having meetings:

- Introduction: Show the managers/teams available film clip of the Solomon Asch experiments to illustrate the power of conformity. Inform them that 1/3 conform. Ask the participants to share how this is playing out in their own group or in those the lead or participate in.

- Inform the participants that our good intentions to verbally encourage others and each other to speak up and share our views, also when we do not agree is not enough to prohibit group conformity and leverages diversity of perspectives to apply in the task-solving process or decision-making process.

- Share these "PROCESS" Inclusion Nudge examples with the participants and afterwards ask them to design some more based on their experience:

  - SHARE IN WRITING: Ask all team members to write their perspective or critical view on a note. Place all notes in a pile and have one team member read them out loud (S. Asch experiment shows that conformity drops 2/3). Team members elaborate on their perspectives if necessary. If working virtually, post perspectives in the virtual meeting room wall, and have the facilitator read them out loud.

  - ARGUE FOR THE OTHER: Ask all team members to find one or more argument(s) that support another team member's arguments even when not agreeing.
  - SHARE WITH ALLY: Share perspectives in pairs

  - SHARE EACH OTHER'S PERSPECTIVES: Share perspectives in pairs and then tell each other's perspectives to the larger group.

- SILENT SENSE CHECK OF DECISION: Having made a decision, ask all participants to write down what they understand has just been decided (this should be anonymous). Ask one person to read all the notes out loud. Often the content turns out to be different from what people understood. Always allow extra time for a decision-making process to make sure everyone is aligned and has understood the same thing.

- Ask participants: *"When the group dynamic of conformity happens in all groups, what will you do proactively to change this?"* Instruct the participants in groups to come up with ways of working that will help the group to be inclusive and leverage the full potential of the group, and prevent the negative impact of these group mechanisms.

Impact

- Actions designed to tweak the process in facilitation, collaboration, task-solving and decision-making to leverage diversity of perspectives and reduce the negative impact of unconscious patterns and group dynamics
- Motivation to change behaviour and ways of working
- A shared commitment to leverage the diverse perspectives in a group

Authors' Comments

This is ideal to use in business planning sessions, team development sessions, LEAN processes (LEAN Board meetings) or leadership team meetings. You can teach the manager to facilitate this. By implementing ways of working that automatically leverage diversity of thought, you do not rely only on awareness, reflection, or extroverts. The majority of people having gone through this process apply these Inclusion Nudges and involve their teams in doing the same.

"PROCESS" Inclusion Nudge:

JOB INTERVIEW IN TWO PARTS REDUCING IMPACT OF ASSUMPTIONS

Submitted by: Tinna C. Nielsen, Founder of Move the Elephant for Inclusiveness

Why

We are often seduced by those who are culturally recognisable, who fit the organisational norm and the norm for how to behave in a job-interview (also culturally specific). Research shows that we ask such candidates less critical questions, but more guide and encouraging micro-gestures, while failing to guide those we instinctively rate as no-candidates, thereby giving them poor opportunity to perform in the interview. It is a challenge to change this during the interview because this is happening in the unconscious automatic system of the brain.

The Inclusion Nudge

Split the job interview into two parts. The second part of the interview is a brief evaluation with the candidate. This Inclusion Nudge makes it easier to challenge assumptions about the candidate because the recruitment panel get a second chance to talk to them and seek out facts to counter the assumptions/stereotypes/biases etc. This simple intervention as part of the existing process makes the process and decision-making less biased, and improves the comparison of the candidates after the interview process.

How

- Inform the candidates about the process beforehand.

- Part one is the regular interview. Shorten this by 10 minutes.

- Mid-way evaluation: The recruiter and the diverse recruiting team leave the room and make an immediate five-minute evaluation of strong and weak sides, questions they didn't ask (re: the screening criteria) or answers they didn't get. They also flag implicit associations to each other and challenge these by asking questions like *"If 'he' was a 'she' would we have thought the same?"*, or *"If he had not had a two-year break, would we have…?"*, or *"If he didn't have such a soft voice, would we have listened differently?"*, *"If she had the same education as me, would I have…?"*.

- Part two is a short (10 minute) evaluation with the candidate.

- Final evaluation: The recruiting team makes the final evaluation without the candidate.

- The recruiting team discusses the rejection arguments in relation to the selection and screening criteria.

You should inform candidates that the interview will be conducted in two parts. Be sure to apply this approach to all interviews for the same position.

Impact

- Many hiring managers report that the process makes a difference because they often experience it is like meeting a different person/candidate in the second part of the interview (now they know each other, not so uncomfortable, the candidate is less nervous) and that their first immediate perception of the candidate changes.

- The intervention helps the brain shift mode of thinking: Raises the level of reflection on emotional-oriented / biased associations.

- Reduces the tendency to primarily consider information that tends to confirm assumptions.

- Reduces the risk of being seduced by candidates who are good at interviews, and gives a second chance to ask critical questions.

- Improves the ground for comparison after the final evaluations of all candidates.

"PROCESS" Inclusion Nudge:

"OBSERVER PAUSE BUTTON" IN HIPO SELECTION PROCESS

Submitted by: Suzanne Price, Founder of Price Global

Why

Senior leaders were not nominating eligible female talent for high potential (HiPo) programmes and high-visibility projects at the same rate as male talent.

The Inclusion Nudge

Bring in a neutral observer in HiPo selection meetings to *"hit the pause button"* and give feedback on bias or assumptions in the evaluation and selection process.

How

Before the selection meeting, HR analysed the statistics on percentages of female and male talent eligible for the high-potential programme. It appeared that while 80% of eligible males were selected, only 40% of eligible females were.

Suzanne was invited to join the selection meetings as a neutral consultant. Being from the outside, she did not know any of the candidates.

- The senior leaders allocated twice as much time as usual for this meeting.

- Suzanne's role was to pause the meeting anytime she believed it would be beneficial to slow down the process and provide feedback to the senior leaders so that they might revisit what they had decided.

  ○ Examples included a woman considered to lead a highly visible project. One of the senior leaders said, "No, she has a soft voice." Then all moved onto the next candidate. Suzanne asked if anyone noticed what had just happened. They had not. She mirrored back the words they used and their decision to eliminate a candidate because of her soft voice. Without further explanation, the senior leaders realised they could have stalled her career because of a perception about her voice.

o   The next step was to consider the female candidate again. This time she was selected, and it was suggested that she should be supported with a few coaching sessions on how to amplify her presence in a male-dominated organisation.

Impact

Senior leaders realised some potential bias in the selection process and became more willing to reconsider potential female candidates. The number of women nominated doubled from three to six, and four were promoted during the annual cycle.

Authors' Comments

This first serves as a "FEEL THE NEED" Inclusion Nudge, much like the example from Charlotte Sweeney, where the unreflected is called out. In this case, it is addressed in the moment and causes a pause in the process. This may be an "eye opener" experience at first, and hence serve as a "FEEL THE NEED" Inclusion Nudge. The "PROCESS" Inclusion Nudge is by having a neutral observer built into the meeting design and also the "pause" in the process where the feedback on potentially biased comments were given to the group in the moment and discussed.

"PROCESS" Inclusion Nudge:

BALANCING OPPORTUNITIES FOR IN-GROUP / OUT-GROUP

Submitted by: Vernā Myers, Vernā Myers Consulting Group
The Authors have added additional content.

Why

The In-Group/Out-Group Dynamic can have profound implications in workplaces on areas such as information sharing, assignment of key projects, visibility, decision-making and promotion. Since we have a strong bias in favour of those we perceive to be like us, these people become our "go-to people". We tend to trust their input more and interact with them at higher levels than those who are in our "Out-Group". This happens on an automatic level and can place a real challenge on inclusion when not examined. It becomes especially complicated when a team manager has "In-Group" members on her/his work team. In this case, a manager may not be aware of the "In-Group" dynamic and may find rational reasons to always favour these individuals. For a balanced distribution of opportunities for all on the team, nudges can help make the invisible more visible, and thus shift behaviour to be more inclusive.

Two Inclusion Nudges

- Use the entire list when determining whom to choose for an opportunity.
- Rotate opportunities.

How

For any project assignments, build into the process an Inclusion Nudge to aim to not "automatically" select the person to assign the project, but establish a process of consulting a list.

- Do this formally by creating a checklist to be completed for all project assignments which would cover key information such as project description, resources needed, timeline, stakeholders, etc., and also the nudging question at the top of the checklist asking *"Have I looked at the entire list of people who are eligible to lead this project?"*

- This can be taken one step further by adding in a statement of intentionality, such as *"As an inclusive leader, I want to ensure that all edible team members have equal and fair opportunities. One step I will do is rotating projects across all eligible people on the team."* Intentional statements increase our commitment to action by nearly 50% more than not writing down and reading these.

By looking at the entire list of people who are eligible, then we don't use our mental list, which is corrupted with our own "In-Group" of people with whom we feel comfortable. If you rely only on them we will miss someone who is capable but not in our circle.

Another variant on this is if you are a manager or lead a group of people, make sure to find ways (numbers, pick out of the hat, alpha or birth order) to rotate tasks and opportunities (speaking roles, responsibilities, note taking, conferences, writing articles) so that everyone gets a chance. The Inclusion Nudge to accomplish this good practice is to have a question on the top of a "Task List" or "To Do List", such as *"Share the tasks with all equally."* This will move the automatic thinking of *"who?"* to the reflective thinking of *"who else?"*.

Impact

By forcing the distribution of opportunities, we can rely less on our brains to consider others who should be involved. We are thus more inclusive with less effort.

"PROCESS" Inclusion Nudge:

MAKING BEST USE OF YOUR HIGH POTENTIALS

Submitted by: Veronika Hucke, D&I Strategy & Solutions

Why

As part of the talent management process, many organizations use a standard nine box Performance / Potential grid. This does not mean, though, that people identified as the highest performance / potential talents necessarily have the same opportunity to advance: Regularly, "diverse talents" – those not belonging to the majority population – are as likely as majority talent to be placed in the top three grid boxes but are less likely to be included in succession plans for more senior roles.

The Inclusion Nudge

Make it a requirement that all diverse talents that meet relevant criteria – e.g. grid placement – are indeed on a succession plan.

How

As part of your talent review / succession planning process, clearly communicate expectations and guidelines to ensure that diverse talents are being leveraged and considered for succession. Implement transparent metrics to ensure target achievement. Also remember to implement a regular review of "success rates" of identified successors to make sure that diverse candidates are not being added randomly to succession plans just to tick a box.

Results

This process ensures that more attention is given to diverse talents which often are not located in the "center of power" making it more likely for them to be overlooked. This increased attention broadens the candidate pool and ensures that performance and potential are core factors for advancement, rather than knowing the right people, resulting in more diverse succession plans. Due to process flow it is unlikely that a 100% target is achieved in the first year, providing an opportunity for follow up and identifying uncharted barriers to diverse talents becoming succession candidates that can be addressed as practices evolve.

"PROCESS" Inclusion Nudge:

INSTANT PERFORMANCE FEEDBACK

Submitted by: Lisa Kepinski, Founder, Inclusion Institute

Why

Research consistently shows that the traditional annual performance review does not work for many employees, especially for Generation X and Y and the incoming Generation Z. The challenge is that the traditional review system is intended to focus on the entire past year, but Recency Bias (sometimes called Halo/Horns Bias) often kicks in so that only the most recent accomplishments or failures are remembered. Also, studies have shown that the annual performance review triggers a "fight or flight" reaction in employees, which interferes with hearing feedback and feeling motivation to change behaviour. Many companies have decided it was easier to change the system than to achieve the desired behaviour change within the existing process.

The Inclusion Nudge

By using automated, real-time communications tools, which are similar to social media approaches, employees can receive instant feedback from multiple sources on their performance. For example: "Great presentation in the meeting today" or a simple "Like" indicator). This nudge of immediate feedback helps change or reinforces desired behaviour.

How

Approaches vary across companies, but many now rely on instant performance feedback systems that are either in-house designed or purchased from an external partner. These usually give both the opportunity for immediate feedback, and also have an archive feature which can be reviewed for a comprehensive look on performance, if the organisation is still conducting annual or semi-annual performance appraisals.

 © T. Nielsen & L. Kepinski, 2016
www.inclusion-nudges.org

Impact

The system in place tags the feedback comments to the employee's journal or file, which helps counter Recency Bias. It also helps motivate employees who value immediate feedback and helps steer their behaviour in a timely manner. Overall, it equips managers to make smarter decisions that improve performance, productivity and talent retention, while equipping employees with the information needed to assess their performance and deliver their best.

Authors' Comments

This Inclusion Nudge was inspired by several books, research studies and articles, plus experience in organisations showing that the annual performance process was not working effectively. Across many sectors, we are seeing companies replace or significantly modify their annual performance review process (including Microsoft, Adobe, Expedia, Twilio, and Motorola). The purpose of a performance review system is to improve behaviour to support the organisation's goals and increase employee satisfaction. Organisations are finding that the feedback loop is one key area in which they can implement change and better fit with the workforce of today and tomorrow. We see this area as an excellent space to design nudges

"PROCESS" Inclusion Nudge:

REFRAMING ALL TALENTS AS "READY NOW" IN SUCCESSION PLANNING

Submitted by: Sue Johnson, Nestle, Global Head of D&I

Why

We all have thinking tendencies (biases) such as seeking out information to support what we already believe (confirmation bias) and over-valuing information we receive early on in an evaluation (anchoring and the halo effect). We also tend to rate recent performance more highly than earlier performance. This results in unequal evaluations, thus unequal opportunities for career opportunities and a loss of performance potential in the organisation.

The Inclusion Nudge

Change the default in most organisations from *"When is the candidate ready?"* to *"The candidate is ready now."* Then managers have to argue *"Why not?"* (opt out) instead of *"Why?"* (opt in). This shifts the mode of thinking, promoting more objective evaluations.

How

Implement this in successor evaluation meetings (ready now) or performance-calibration meetings (start with the highest rating).

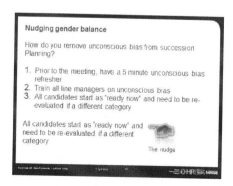

© T. Nielsen & L. Kepinski, 2016
www.inclusion-nudges.org

Authors' Comments

Nestlé uses this Inclusion Nudge to focus on promoting gender balance in succession planning. We believe it also has the potential to reduce biases about nationality, personality, communication style, age, and more – thereby increasing diversity broadly in leadership/talent pipelines. Similar changes in the default have been applied in the education system changing the grade system to all pupils starting with the highest grade. See the RSA research findings in *"Everyone starts with an A"* on how this narrowed performance gaps and socioeconomic attainment gaps.

"PROCESS" Inclusion Nudges

SECTION SUMMARY

Keep in mind that the purpose of "PROCESS" Inclusion Nudge are to are intended to help people *make better decisions and leverage diversity*. This is done by altering elements of such organisational processes as candidate screening, promotions, performance reviews and successor planning. It also involves collaborative processes like meetings and facilitation. These behavioural interventions also promotes a more reflective process in as we follow or engage with our organisation's established processes and systems and as we interact with others in accomplishing work.

See Section 6 for information on designing "PROCESS" Inclusion Nudges.

© T. Nielsen & L. Kepinski, 2016
www.inclusion-nudges.org

Section 5: EXAMPLES OF "FRAMING" INCLUSION NUDGES

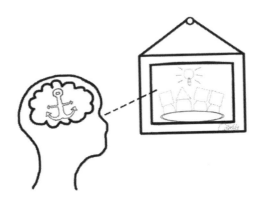

Reminder:
"FRAMING" Inclusion Nudges are intended to help people (the brain) *perceive issues related to inclusion, diversity, equality in a resource discourse, and to prime specific associations and thus inclusive behaviours* by altering the frame or change the anchor of the thought process.

Note: Many "FRAMING" Inclusion Nudges are often an integrated "PROCESS" Inclusion Nudges, since they can be an integrated part of organisational processes or ways of working.

Inspirational Thoughts

"Framing works because people tend to be somewhat mindless passive decision makers. Their Reflective System does not do the work that would be required to check and see whether reframing the questions would produce a different answer." – **Thaler & Sustein**

"If you change the way you look at things, the things you look at change." – **Wayne Dyer**

"Even if the frame provides no substantive information, it can change people's preferences and choices. This is especially true if the frame is positive. Because of loss aversion, simply framing a choice option in a positive light will increase the chances of something being chosen. The package is more important than substance." – **Morris Altman**

"...The mind doesn't search for information in a vacuum. Rather it starts by using whatever information is immediately available as a reference point or 'anchor' and then adjusting." – **Banaji & Greenwald**

Inspirational Thoughts *Continued*

*"Symbols and other meaningful images have the capacity to quickly inspire extreme reactions, ranging from anger and fear to joy and celebrations. They're especially powerful because we process symbolic images very quickly—more quickly than we process the meaning of words—and they correspondingly embed themselves more deeply in our memories. Symbols, then, are magnets for meaning, and they have the power to shape our thoughts and behaviours just as words and labels do." – **Adam Alter**

*"Another heuristic involves Anchoring. No piece of information is processed in isolation. Mental patterns are contagious, and everything is judged in comparison to something else. ... Then there is framing. Every decision gets framed within a certain linguistic context. If a surgeon tells his patients that a procedure may have a 15% failure rate, they are likely to decide against it. If he tells them the procedure has an 85% success rate, they tend to opt for it." – **David Brooks**

"FRAMING" Inclusion Nudge:

REFRAME A QUESTION INCREASE THE NUMBER OF WOMEN ON INTERNATIONAL ASSIGNMENTS

Submitted by: Lisa Kepinski, Founder, Inclusion Institute

Why

In many organisations significantly more men than women receive international assignments, which are seen as a required career experience for promotion to senior roles. This pattern and implicit norm sharply narrows the pipeline of internal women for senior executive roles. There is a need to widen this pipeline to be more gender balanced. The first step is to get women to answer *"yes"* to the question, *"Are you internationally mobile?"* in i.e. the on boarding process in the system or in the performance review/appraisal process. The challenge is that men and women do not perceive questions the same way. Research also shows that words appeal differently to men and women, and to people with other differences. The challenge is also that 'International mobile' often is perceived as a total relocation, which has consequences for the employees' family.

The Inclusion Nudge

By changing a seemingly neutral question about international mobility, the anchor of the thought process was changed. As a result, data about men and women's interest in international assignments was more accurate. To ensure that the perception of the question by both genders was more closely aligned, the wording of the question was changed from:

> *"Will you take an international assignment?"* or *"Are you international mobile?"*

> to

> *"Will you consider an international assignment at some point in the future?".*

How

Extensive organisational and external research was conducted to reveal potential for gender bias in the employee life cycle and organisational culture. Results showed that the first trigger for an international assignment rested with the employee's answer to one question in their online talent profile: *"Will you take an international assignment?"*

Research showed that women tended to answer *"no"* due to reflection about the current moment, especially thoughts of home and life demands *("How will I ever get everything arranged? So much is depending on me to be here and available.")*. Men, however, tended to answer *"yes"* *("I'll sort it out when the time comes. There's no firm offer right now.")*.

The "FRAMING" Inclusion Nudge we put in place was to change the question to *"Will you consider an international assignment at some point in the future?"*

Impact

By simply reframing one question, more women (more than a 25% increase in one year) said they would consider an international assignment. It's not that 25% more women were all of a sudden international mobile, but that 25% more women answered yes, due to a change in perception of the implications of answering yes. It can be assumed that in this case women answer the original question from a present frame of reference, thinking about the consequences on the private front, thus being more reluctant. Whereas men would answer from a future frame of reference, thinking this could work out when there is an actual offer later on. And it can also be assumed that men would answer yes based on insights that being registered as international mobile would further their career opportunities (in alignment with men applying when they master about 60% of the required skills for a job and women when mastering 100%).

Authors' Comments

This Inclusion Nudge was designed by Lisa when she worked as an internal I&D leader in a multinational corporation, but reframing a seemingly neutral question like this, is applicable in all organisations because they will all be fighting for skilled talent in a global workforce. One critical trend in the labour market is an increased demand for highly skilled workers and a shortage in the future. This means that also organisations with a domestic orientation will need to make themselves attractive to skilled talent across borders. Questions like *"Would you be agile to work on international assignments for shorter periods of time?"* or *"Would you consider commuting to work in various locations?"* could be relevant. We recommend that you experiment with the powerful technique of reframing seemingly neutral questions in as many organisational areas as possible.

© T. Nielsen & L. Kepinski, 2016
www.inclusion-nudges.org

"FRAMING" Inclusion Nudge:

FROM MAXIMUM TO MINIMUM REQUIREMENTS

Submitted by: Veronika Hucke, D&I Strategy & Solutions

Why

Research consistently shows that women make "safer" choices in job applications and need to feel comfortable about considerably more of the requirements than men do: Women apply if they believe they meet at least 85% of job requirements, while men apply if they meet between 40% and 60% of the criteria.

The Inclusion Nudge

To achieve a more gender balanced applicant pool, focus job postings on the most essential job requirements rather than a very long list of "nice to haves".

How

Ensure that job postings have a maximum of about five requirements defined – either via the settings of the recruitment system or clear specifications for job postings.

Impact

Increases share of female applicants, as they feel more confident about meeting the requirements of the role.

Authors' Comments

This Inclusion Nudge crosses over into two types. It is primarily a "FRAMING" Inclusion Nudge, where the purpose is to change the anchor of the thought process of women to make them apply. Secondly, it is an integrated part of the organisational process of defining positions and writing job adverts, and as such is also a "PROCESS" Inclusion Nudge.

"FRAMING" Inclusion Nudge:

SPECIFY "FEMALE OR MALE" IN JOB POSTINGS

Submitted by: Alberto Platz, VP Global Talent & Engagement, D. Swarovski
Corporation AG

Why

To increase the number of female candidates responding to a job offer or when
applying for a position. In many cases only male candidates applied; it turns out
that women weren't attracted because the wording of job offers sounded
unconsciously masculine.

The Inclusion Nudge

Specify "female or male" in the titles of all job postings. The purpose is to appeal
to both genders, and to open the thinking of the hiring manager to ensure that
both men and women are considered for the role.

How

Revise all job offer texts to include both genders in the titles and descriptions.
For example:

In a sentence: "We are looking for a *female or male* motivated talent."
As a title in the advertisement: *Female or Male* Head of Business
Support

Note: This can also be done for other categories that require balance, including
age, race, disabilities, religion, sexual orientation and nationality.

Swarovski is the first choice of designers.
Swarovski is the first choice of professionals.
Swarovski will be your first choice for success.

Are you interested in developing sound business plans? Can you see yourself
promoting the successful achievement of sales goals? If so, take the opportunity
to apply to one of the world's best-known brands as

HEAD OF CUSTOMER SERVICE EUROPE SOUTH (F/M)
Location:Location: Triesen (Liechtenstein)

Impact

Opening up the minds of managers to focus on both women and men as
applicants (see also the "FEEL THE NEED" Nudge from Alberto Platz on creating
buy-in and motivation for this Inclusion Nudge).

Authors' Comments

This is an example that crosses two types of Inclusion Nudges. It is a "FRAMING"
Inclusion Nudge, where the main purpose is to change the anchor of the thought
process and associations to specific jobs/positions. This is also a "PROCESS"
Inclusion Nudge as it is an integrated part of the organisational process of writing
job adverts.

 © T. Nielsen & L. Kepinski, 2016
www.inclusion-nudges.org

"FRAMING" Inclusion Nudge:

DIFFERENCE AS A CRITERION FOR SELECTION, NOT DE-SELECTION

Submitted by: Janina Norton, Employee Engagement Manager, Company Anonymous

Why

There is a well-known unconscious bias (sometimes referred to as "mini-me syndrome") that can influence recruitment decisions, whereby we tend to prefer candidates similar to ourselves. This bias can prevent a company from selecting the best candidates and benefiting from the recruitment of a diverse mix of thinking styles, capabilities and life experiences.

The Inclusion Nudge

As an integrated part of the selection of candidates at the beginning of the recruitment process, have recruiters ask the hiring manager questions to prod difference as a selection criterion. After the interview, check for patterns in differences among candidate, manager and team.

How

Ideally, all recruiters and hiring managers within an organisation should first undertake awareness sessions on unconscious bias, so they are open to the possibility that they may make unconsciously biased decisions during recruitment.

Before advertising, the hiring manager and recruiter meet to discuss the approach that will be taken to recruit. There is usually already a formal set of questions for this conversation, to discuss what attributes, skills and experience the ideal candidate will have. An additional area of questioning is added to this briefing questionnaire. The recruiter asks the hiring manager such questions as,

"What attributes or traits do you not have, that it would be ideal for the new candidate to have?"

 © T. Nielsen & L. Kepinski, 2016
www.inclusion-nudges.org

The recruiter can, for example, say that the candidate should be detail-oriented, if the manager is a big-picture thinker. Or:

"What traits would be useful for the candidate to have that don't 'fit' with the current team, which might mix things up and create more diverse perspectives?"

After the interview, the original briefing document can be revisited and the recruiter can question the manager on whether the candidate has different traits than the team currently has, that would benefit the team.

Impact

Adding a process change at the stage before short-listing and interviewing provides an opportunity for the hiring manager to reflect on how a different perspective or life experience could benefit the team. This can help managers challenge themselves to find these differences. It also provides an anchor for the recruiter when supporting the hiring manager to make the selection decision: does this new candidate deliver a different style of working, a different set of life experiences or a way of thinking that is currently missing within the team? It makes the individual candidate's differences a criterion for selection, rather than the opposite.

Authors' Comments

To further strengthen this inclusion nudge make the patterns of 'de-selection' arguments and 'selection' arguments from previous recruitment processes visible, i.e. in a template or list and have the managers actively make mark to make their own pattern visible. View and discuss possible implications of their pattern.

"FRAMING" Inclusion Nudge:

ENCOURAGING WOMEN TO APPLY FOR PROMOTIONAL OPPORTUNITIES

Submitted by: Howard Ross, Founder & Chief Learning Officer, Cook Ross Inc.
Based upon a practice conducted by one of his global corporate clients.

Why

Many women tend to hold back from expressing interest and/or applying for a promotional opportunity. They are less likely than their male counterparts to step forward and say that they would be interested in a higher-level role and when such a position does become available, many women often hold back from submitting an application. Research repeatedly shows that women usually feel that they are lacking the full set of needed qualifications in order to be seriously considered for the role. This is sometimes summarized in the many research studies as women feel like they need between 80 to 100% of the job requirements in order to apply and men feel like they need only 30 to 50% of the job requirements in order to apply. The challenge is how to equalize the perception of one's suitability for a position in such a way that a gender-mixed talent pool of applicants is the result.

The Inclusion Nudge

When a job position became open and was announced, a summary of the research findings about women not or under applying and men over applying was also send out as part of the packet of information on the position. The purpose is to shed light on the different ways that women and men view themselves when considering applying for a position, in order to change the anchor of the thought process and to produce more reflective thinking on one's own behaviour and beliefs and how this may impact their career goals.

How

This client company of Cook Ross is led by a very innovative HR leader who wanted to bring greater gender balance across all levels and areas in the company. The company is known for a very talented and educated workforce.

So, tapping into the organisational culture which valued research and inquisitive thinking in order to influence behavioural change, the job announcement process was changed such that when a position became open, a summary of the research findings about women not or under applying and men over applying was also send out as part of the packet of information on the position.

Impact

There have been a greater number of women applying for positions within the company.

Authors' Comments:

Many times there are some small overlaps between "FRAMING" and "PROCESS" Inclusion Nudges. For example with this Inclusion Nudge, it can be perceived as falling into two categories. Primarily, it is a "FRAMING" Inclusion Nudge as the main purpose is to change the anchor of the thought process and create a different association when seeing the job advertisement. While from the organisational practices side, it is a "PROCESS" Inclusion Nudge as it is a change in the process of how position opportunities are announced within the organisation. The behavioural impact is the same for both...seeking a more gender-balanced applicant pool for internal position openings. The type of nudge reflects where the focus/action is taking place...on the individual or the system/process level. And in examples such as this one, a nudge targeting both levels is useful to achieving the behavioural shift.

"FRAMING" Inclusion Nudge:

STATEMENT TRIGGERING REFLECTED THINKING WHEN EVALUATING APPLICANTS

Submitted by: Jo Ann Morris, Owner and Principal, Integral Coaching LLC

Why

Research and experience have firmly shown that, despite our best intentions for equity, our automatic reactions when we view faces and read names can be contrary to our conscious intentions. Implicit associations are powerful, especially when not noticed, which can lead to faulty decision-making based on bias, especially in interviews. It takes concentrated effort to work again biases like homophily — hiring only people who are like us or who closely fit the organisation's majority or leadership culture.

The Inclusion Nudge

Present interviewers with the statement "*I will notice my reaction to the names I read and to the faces I see*" on their computer screen before they review resumes of applicants for a position, in order to trigger the unreflected to become reflected.

How

- First conduct a session on unconscious bias and ways this can interfere with our judgments of others.
- As a follow-up for those involved in hiring, set up a personal message that triggers greater attention to bias. Fifteen minutes before an interview or scheduled time to review resumes for an open position, the hiring manager and team receive a reminder message on their computer with the statement, "*I will notice my reaction to the names I read and to the faces I see.*" This is written in very large font and strong colours to stick in the mind. Some also print out the statement and place it in front of them as they review resumes.

o   This message may be done as a calendar appointment by the hiring manager herself/himself, or by a member of the staffing team, or built by IT as an automatic pop up message prior to an interview or review of resumes.

Impact

This statement focuses attention on unreflected behaviour and judgements. Starting the statement "*I will...*" makes this a first step on an individual action level. It is also helpful to have a similar discussion across the hiring team on reactions to names and faces and how this may influence decisions.

"FRAMING" Inclusion Nudge:

A QUESTION CHALLENGING UNREFLECTED EXCLUSION

Submitted by: Vernā Myers, Vernā Myers Consulting Group

Why

We have a strong bias in favour of those who seem like us, and these people become our "go-to people". We tend to trust their input more and interact with them at higher levels than those who are in our "Out-Group". This happens on an automatic level and can be a real challenge to inclusion when not examined. It can be especially complicated when "In-Group" members are comprised of those in the majority or in power (for example replicating leaders). In this case, the "In-Group" becomes invisible to its members and is perceived as *"normal"* or *"just the way things are"*. The In-Group/Out-Group Dynamic can have profound implications on areas such as information sharing, assignment of key projects, visibility, decision-making and promotion. For greater inclusion, Inclusion Nudges can help make the invisible more visible, and thus shift behaviour to be more inclusive.

The Inclusion Nudge

Painted on the wall of a meeting room was the question, *"Is everyone at the table?"*

How

When meeting in this room, the group responds to the question. At first this may be done as a team-process discussion; eventually it will become a habit.

Impact

By forcing the brain to consider others who should be involved in the discussion, we are more open to inclusion.

Authors' Comments

This example was shared by Vernā Myers based on one of her clients. It is a great example of how a simple question can trigger reflection. It this though also a question with an inherent risk of being answered with a 'yes' due to blindness to any kind of exclusion. We recommend you to experiment with a 'loss-aversion' trigger by posing the question *"Who's not at the table? What could we be missing out on?"* Since human behaviour is driven more by what we lose. We are twice as miserable about what we lose as we are gaining the exact same.

This visible question could furthermore be supplemented with showing the awareness test "WHODUNNIT" on selective attention[34]. The point is that there are things we don't see, but with diverse perspectives we see other things and potentially more. The conference room computers could be set up to have this as default start up. People will see the test many times then, but very few will ever see the 21 changes – it could become a competition over time to spot as many changes as possible.

"FRAMING" Inclusion Nudge:

MAXIMUM 70% HOMOGENEITY TEAM TARGET

Submitted By: Tinna C. Nielsen, Founder, Move the Elephant for Inclusiveness;
and Susanne Justesen, Ph.D. and Innovation-Diversity Advisor, Innoversity
Copenhagen

Why

We know from research[35] that too much homogeneity or sameness in a group directly impacts performance, measured on the groups' ability to solve problems, make decisions, reach their deadlines, maintain their budgets, and not least of all, their overall economic performance. Based on a study conducted among 469 teams[36] we learned, that the direct link between performance and group homogeneity was the strongest when homogeneity of nationality, gender, or age-group (generation) did not exceed 70% in the groups measured. That is, group performance became negatively impacted when more than 70% of group members had the same gender, the same nationality and/or belonged to the same age-group. The same results was found in research on the 'Critical mass of 30%' from the 1970's and in research on releasing innovative potential in team by London Business School – they found that 50:50 on gender had the biggest impact[37].

Classical diversity dimensions tend to trigger unconscious associations such as:

"Gender = Women = Women's Issue = Helping Women = Women Instead of the Most Competent"

The connotations of such words will not lead the thought process to:

"Diversity = All of Us"

Often the connotations of target setting such as 30% women in leadership are of a moral character with associations of *"nice to have"*. To avoid affirmative action in reaching targets for diversity, an approach that generates associations with business rationality is needed:

"Inclusion & Diversity = Performance"

The Inclusion Nudge proposed here therefore helps people think about the *"problems of homogeneity"* rather than the *"virtues of diversity"*, thereby turning the diversity agenda away from being *"nice-to-have"* towards rather a *"need-to-have"*.

The Inclusion Nudge

A 'Maximum 70% Homogeneity' team target.

Set a team composition target instead of a target for diversity - you set a target for high performance and innovation Reframe the targets to be about reducing homogeneity and set a target for the maximum similarity of various demographic factors.

This has been the team composition objective in Arla Foods since 2010.

Max. 70% of team members with the same **national / ethnic background**

Max. 70% of team members with the same **gender**

Max. 70% of team members from the same **generation**

Max. 70% of team members from the same **educational/professional background**

How

- When you cluster gender with such other differences as nationality and age, you avoid associations to women being "the problem to fix".

- Differentiate the objective to be realistic in accordance with the current pipeline and hierarchical levels. For example the Executive Management Group and Business Group's Top Leadership teams have to reach the objective in all four factors. Other leadership teams and employee teams (including project teams) have to reach the objective in at least two factors and more if possible (if in the available recruitment base). This differentiated team objective was set in Arla Foods.

- Create a simple assessment tool for managers: a one-page Excel spreadsheet to assess the percentage of the dominant gender, nationality, generation, educational/professional background. Or use the 70% Homogeneity Quick Test available via Innoversity Academy.[38]

- The objective does not have to be mandatory nor linked to bonuses to work. Create motivation and buy-in from leaders by showing research results and internal data that demonstrate the correlation between team composition and performance[39]. Use some of the "FEEL THE NEED" Inclusion Nudges to motivate (such as the 'Resume-exercise' or the 'Warmth-Competency-exercise'). Create a "Follow the Herd" reaction by showcasing that the majority of "similar others" are reaching this target, *"7 out of 10 teams in your unit"*.

- If you would like to learn about other organisations pursuing the Max 70% Homogeneity Principle, you can read about their experiences and none the least about The Max 70% Homogeneity Club (launching in spring 2015); a members only initiative for leaders who have decided to strategically pursue the 70% principle for all team and project groups within their organisation.

Impact

The performance diversity measures behind the 'max 70% principle' relates to teams only (when there is direct collaboration amongst the group members in question). Research shows that when the prevalence of demographic factors such as gender, generation, and nationality is set at a maximum of 70% on a team, performance is better (profit margin on average 3.7% higher in diverse teams vs more homogeneous teams) than in teams with a higher prevalence of these factors[40].

By changing targets for the representation of demographic diversity in teams, the perception and thus the conversation about Inclusion & Diversity in Arla Foods changed to be predominantly resource and performance oriented. This discourse change was driven by those who had participated in the I&D learning sessions (bottom-up change movement). There has been minimal resistance from leaders – on the contrary, leaders express explicit support for such target setting because it resonates with performance and innovation.

Leaders in Arla Foods use the objective as a guiding principle in recruitment, restructuring of teams, staffing project teams, and composing work groups (no accountability). They report positive group dynamics and better performance in the diverse teams.

"FRAMING" Inclusion Nudge:

REQUIRE DISCONFIRMING DATA TO CHALLENGE BIASED DECISIONS ON INTERNAL MINORITY CANDIDATES

Submitted by: Vernā Myers, Vernā Myers Consulting Group

Why

Most organisations with an I&D program want to increase diversity at all levels. This is often expressed as increasing the number of women, but in the U.S. it also refers to increasing numbers of people of colour, especially in senior positions. Efforts have included widening the talent pool, engaging with specialized search agencies, improving employer branding campaigns, establishing internal targets with senior executives reviewing for progress, leadership development training and mentoring. Despite these actions, movement remains slow in most organisations. The intentions are good, but often actions simply reinforce the existing demographic structure. Clearly we need an approach that involves the unconscious mind, which can be pivotal in maintaining the status quo and resisting change.

The Inclusion Nudge

Requiring data disconfirming the decision when a diversity candidate is *not* being recommended for promotion.

How

If a woman or person of colour was not among those recommended for promotion when a senior-level opportunity opened up, the manager would be required by agreement from the CEO/executive leadership team to go back and find as much data as possible that would disaffirm the decision not to promote a diverse person and report back to the executive management team.

Impact

This process provides a second look at assumptions and decisions – some of which may have been unconscious and unreflected. Without talking about bias it can be possible to mitigate the impact of unconscious bias.

Authors' Comments

This example was shared by Vernā Myers and is based on her discussions with a business professor who had tried it with senior leaders. While this Inclusion Nudge is written from a U.S. context of gender and race, it could be applied to any area of diverse hiring around the world.

Other organisations use similar interventions of *"IF NOT, WHY NOT?"* reporting. This involves if a 'non-majority' candidate is not hired/promoted, then the hiring manager reports to hers/his senior leader of the business unit with arguments *'WHY NOT?'* and *'WHY WAS THE 'USUAL' MAJORITY CANDIDATE SELECTED?'*. The awareness of the procedure itself is the anchor of a more reflected thought process, more than is the actual reporting.

"FRAMING" Inclusion Nudge:

MAJORITY DATA FIRST & HUMANISE THE NUMBERS

Submitted by: Lisa Kepinski, Founder, Inclusion Institute

Why

Too often only the minority data is reported on organisational scorecards. Also, the mind becomes accustomed to seeing small figures associated with "minority" populations. Small numbers associated with a group of people can have an unconscious connection to "less worth". This can limit the urgency and action that leaders may take when reviewing diversity scorecards. Second, the mind can become too accustomed to seeing numbers as numbers and forget that with inclusion, we are focused on people – all of us.

Two Inclusion Nudges

1. In all I&D related data reports, list data *both* for the majority *and* the minority. This provides a complete picture.

2. If possible, use pictures to illustrate the people, for example of the High Potential pool or of the leaders at Partner level or members of the Board/Executive leadership team. Humanising the numbers change perceptions.

How

- With all I&D related data reports, list data for *both* majority *and* minority. This provides a complete picture.
  - List the majority data first.
  - It can be more jarring to see that 90% of senior executives are men than to see that 10% are women. It is easier to explain away the 10% than the 90%.
- With hiring data reports, show both the actual number and percentage for *both* majority *and* minority that were hired in a reporting period.

- o If only showing minority, as most organisations do to measure against a diversity hiring goal, then the bigger picture is overlooked as don't have the full context on the total numbers of all hires that were made during that period. Thus, the data doesn't open the discussion on "missed opportunities" to have hired more non-majority candidates and why this happened.
- This "full reporting" also signals to leaders that efforts must include the majority as well as the minority.
- To humanize the numbers, use photographs to illustrate your point: for example, a group photo of the Executive Leadership Team next to the demographic data at that level. Or, if you are reporting on some groups and they are not present at those levels, build the scorecard to reflect the empty spaces where they could be but aren't.

Impact

Change the framing of the issue by showing the majority first to change the connotation; this anchors the thought process. When I have used this type of reporting, it is a fuller discussion about the organisation. It shifts the view from *"helping the minority"* which can seemingly be a small pocket of people (and as many are *'unseen'* it doesn't feel as *'real'* so photos also help in this regard), to instead become a focus on *"why do we have so many of this population (the majority) at this level or in this business unit?"* It is useful to then discuss implicit associations for "executives" or "sales roles" or "HR" and compare this to the majority data for these areas. Usually there is a direct connection. It is also useful to bring into the discussion the danger of homogenous teams and the potential impact on Group Think, decision making, and business performance.

"FRAMING" Inclusion Nudge:

INCREASE WOMEN IN SALES ROLES BY SHIFTING THEIR PERCEPTION

Submitted by: Lisa Kepinski, Founder, Inclusion Institute
Originated from Lut Nelissen, then the General Western Europe HR Director, Hewlett-Packard, and Lisa was the EMEA D&I Director, Hewlett-Packard

Why

There were less women than men in business customer-facing sales roles in this high tech company. There was an intent to achieve a gender balance in the sales function, and the incoming graduates' intern program was one of the focal points to begin working on this goal. Despite senior leadership, HR, hiring managers, and the sales function all coming together to support this goal, it was seen that women recent university graduates were not expressing interest in a sales internship, despite them having the qualifications and a strong, welcoming internship program from the company to start them off on a good footing in the position.

The Inclusion Nudges

Reframe how the sales role was described in order to help women envision themselves in such a job position or even as a longer-term career focus.

How

- Careful study and inquiries of the women university graduates revealed that they were perceiving the sales role as *"highly masculine, competitive, aggressive"*... more of the outdated 1950's style of business.

- However, in reality, this was no longer the overall nature of sales in this company. Instead it was about *"collaboration, understanding the customer, providing a helping service, seeking a win-win solution."*

 © T. Nielsen & L. Kepinski, 2016
www.inclusion-nudges.org

- To help shift the perception of the women university graduates, the position description was rewritten to include many of the above descriptions to more accurately reflect the role. Also, several successful women and men in sales roles were profiled in supporting material where they described in their own words why they liked their profession, what it was really like, and highlighted the above descriptions. And many of these sales leaders were on hand at job recruiting fairs in universities to be able to immediate respond of any misperceptions on what a sales role is like.

Impact

Change the framing of the what the sales role was being perceived as to more accurately reflect today's dynamics, resulted in more university women graduates signing up to participate in the sales internship program. It was also found that this more accurate picture of a sales role also resonated with some male graduates who also held an outdated view of "sales" and were avoiding inquiring about the internship program.

"FRAMING" Inclusion Nudge:

I&D "WHY NOT?"

Submitted by: Alberto Platz, VP Global Talent & Engagement, D. Swarovski
Corporation AG

Why

To get buy-in for I&D from top management we tend to present lots of business cases, trying to make them understand that I&D should be driven as a business topic, not an ethical topic. It is difficult to find a business case saying anything against I&D. There is no doubt that prioritising I&D is the right thing to do, but it is often not enough to get a full commitment to allocate the needed resources, nor to promote the needed behavioural changes.

The challenge is to find a stronger WHY for I&D. Often that task is given to the head of I&D and/or head of talent or HR, which can result in an HR-focused business case developed within the HR function and often limited by an HR perspective, rather than being developed by business leaders themselves and based on business strategy. It is chiefly at the business leaders level where buy-in is primarily needed. If they aren't on board, it can be significantly challenging, and questionably possible, to accomplish the scope of culture change need for I&D.

The Inclusion Nudge

Position Inclusion & Diversity from the beginning as a "must have" – and ask managers to find reasons to opt out.

How

The Inclusion Nudge is to engage top management in identifying the *"WHY NOT?"* instead of the *"WHY YES?"* for I&D. The purpose is to make managers realize that there is no business case *against* diversity and that inclusiveness has a direct correlation with engagement, thus positive business results.

Impact

If the WHY is strong and top management is convinced based on their own findings and arguments, then they will drive I&D.

© T. Nielsen & L. Kepinski, 2016
www.inclusion-nudges.org

INCLUSION NUDGES

Practical Techniques for Behaviour, Culture, & System Change to Mitigate Unconscious Bias & Create Inclusive Organisations

"FRAMING" Inclusion Nudge:

ALTERNATIVE TO DIVERSITY EXCUSES

Submitted by: Cindy Gallop, Consultant and Speaker, CindyGallop.com, IfWeRanTheWorld.com, and MakeLoveNotPorn.com

Authors' Note: Cindy's reference to this Inclusion Nudge in a TED Talk first came to our attention through an article by Tanya M. Odom, Global Consultant and Leadership Coach [1]

Why

Unfortunately, all too often we hear leaders in organizations make comments such as *'There just isn't any diverse talent available'* or *'Women don't want to work in our industry'* as a reason for lack of progress with increasing diverse representation within the company. This can occur despite a concerted effort on bias awareness training, being shown new ways to find and attract diverse talent, and sharing of demographic data. This can crop up with organisations looking to hire new employees, determine who's in the 'high potential pool', and with promotions to senior leadership roles. The statements of diversity being *'too hard for these types of roles'* or *'not possible in our sector'* cover up a lack of commitment to change...change which would actually benefit the organisation in terms of decision making, financial performance, innovation, and talent. The excuse becomes a blinder or a blocker to increasing diversity and building an inclusive culture.

The Inclusion Nudge

Replace saying *"Diversity is hard"* (or some such excuse given for not working on equity, inclusion, or diversity) with *"I want a homogenous organization (or team)"*.

---

[1] "The Crowd Keynote" by Cindy Gallop, October 5, 2015. Cindy's keynote presentation caught our attention in the article "Trudeau's case for diversity: Because it's 2015" by Tanya M. Odom, CNN online, November 13, 2015 in which Tanya addressed a similar occurrence of 'diversity excuses' when conference speakers and panellists are only from the majority population.

How

With this Inclusion Nudge, the organization needs to have done work on the business case for Inclusion & Diversity, set intentional objectives for increasing diversity representation, offered unconscious bias awareness training, covered the dangers of Group Think and homogeneity, and is committed to finding ways to mitigate bias. Many multinationals usually have had these precursors already accomplished or in play.

Determine a situation to practice this Inclusion Nudge. For example, in a hiring situation, with the interview panel / team, conduct a mini-session reminding the benefits of diversity, the prevalence of bias in decision making, and the negative consequences of Group Think. Then, have the interview team set an agreement to seek out diverse candidates. Each member reads, signs, and states aloud to the group their personal commitment to seek out diverse candidates. Studies show that such action can significantly help reduce bias.

Next, set an interview team agreement that when anyone expresses a comment which may seemingly be a blocker or deterrent to increasing diversity representation in the interview process, that others will reframe the comment and say aloud as something like, *"Are you saying is that you prefer to have a homogenous candidate pool?"* This needs to be done in a neutral, non-punishing way. The goal is to make the unconscious perspective more visible so that it can be countered with a direction more in line with the intentions to increase diversity. It also allows for greater inquisitiveness and problem solving on how to achieve the desired goal.

Impact

This 'FRAMING' Inclusion Nudge raises awareness of automatic excuse-making happening and allows for examination of how such statements are incongruence with our stated intentions of increasing diversity within the company. It offers alternative phrasing of the excuse which calls out the impact of such statements and opens the dialogue for better consideration of information, problem solving, and decision making.

Authors' Comments

This could also be blended with the "PROCES"' Inclusion Nudge "INTERRUPTER" TO PROMOTE OBJECTIVITY IN TALENT DEVELOPMENT DISCUSSIONS by Axel Jentzch at BASF where they ring a bell when a biased statement is made during a talent discussion.

"FRAMING" Inclusion Nudge:

VALUING EMPLOYEE CONTRIBUTIONS TO I&D WORK

Submitted by: Lisa Kepinski, Founder, Inclusion Institute & Veronika Hucke, D&I Strategy & Solutions

Why

Often Inclusion & Diversity (I&D) work in organisations, such as serving as an employee network leader, is seen as "on top of the employee's day job". This mental model of it being "extra work" and not related to one's formal role can result in

> employee involvement in I&D programs not being valued by managers,
> - failing to seeing the wider corporate citizenship contributions that employees can make benefiting the business
> - managers overlooking the learning and development which can come from participation in I&D initiatives

One way that this gets overlooked is by not including employees' contribution to I&D initiatives in their annual performance appraisal. This under-valuing and under-recognition of I&D related contributions by employees has a negative impact on the sustainability of I&D initiatives and also impacts employee engagement.[2]

---

[2] For a specific case study on the negative employee engagement impact of not recognizing the work of women network leaders, see *"A Fresh Look at Women Networks" Global Survey Report*, January 2016, by Veronika Hucke, D&I Strategy & Solutions (http://www.di-strategy.com/research-and-dialogue.html) and Lisa Kepinski, Inclusion Institute (http://www.inclusion-institute.com/what-we-do/research/). Report available via their websites.

The Inclusion Nudge

Insert a prompter question within the performance appraisal process for all employees to ensure that employee contributions to an organisation's I&D strategy are recognised and discussed, and being perceived as everybody's responsibility.

How

Within the performance appraisal process, include standard questions for all employees when they write up their accomplishments and development plans that cover their efforts beyond what is typically described as "their day job". Reframe from the focus of only on the formal role to instead be a wider view of the employee's role *plus* other company-related activities.

The intent is to change the perception of what are "valued" employee contributions to the business and meaningful options for learning & skills development. The reframing question signals to employees and managers that the organisation recognises and rewards employee involvement in company initiatives, such as Inclusion & Diversity, and that such engagement is an advantage for the company. With this 'FRAMING' Inclusion Nudge, we hope to shift the perception of I&D being a 'nice to have' to instead being core to the business and a viable investment of employees' time, which is recognized and rewarded by the organisation's managers.

Examples of questions:

- "In addition to your formal objectives, identify contributions you have done to the make our workplace place more inclusive."
- "How have you helped support making this a great place to work for all employees?"
- "Have you participated in events or served in roles which have offered you new learnings and development?"

While this Inclusion Nudge example is related to I&D, the questions can be written in a broader way that encompasses a wide range of employee contributions to the organisation in other areas such as CSR, community volunteerism, employee and company events, customer-facing product launches, graduate student recruiting fairs, representing the company by speaking at events, and other special projects...all of which are aligned with the organisation's business strategy but are outside of the formal role description or what is typically perceived as one's "day job".

Impact

By integrating such questions into the formal performance appraisal process, it provides a wider view of employees' contributions towards supporting the organisation's goals and culture. It also communicates to employees and managers that I&D is seen as important to the organisation.

Often when being asked how many people are working on I&D, respondents will only consider colleagues that are formally tasked with the role. In that context it is important to highlight that each employee has a role to play to create an inclusive culture.

To be able to realise the potential of all employees contributing towards a more inclusive workplace culture, such beginning points as this 'FRAMING' Inclusion Nudge are needed to help shift the mindset of what are the valued employee contributions.

Authors' Comments

This Inclusion Nudge can also have an impact as a "PROCESS" Inclusion Nudge by changing the performance appraisal objectives setting process to formally include xx% of employees' time to be spent on 'corporate citizenship' or 'corporate culture' work (which could be solely focused on I&D or may be more broad to include I&D, CSR, PR/Brand, etc). This way it is built into the process as part of the formal rewards system and supports creating a more inclusive organisational culture by tasking all employees and managers to do something. To jumpstart such a "PROCESS" Inclusion Nudge as this, there would need to be supporting awareness on what is inclusion, why it's critical to the business, and offering examples of actions which further inclusion plus activities and other ways to get involved in I&D.

"FRAMING" Inclusion Nudge:

REVERSED QUESTIONS TO REDUCE BIAS IN THE MOMENT

Submitted by Gudrun Sander, Director for Diversity and Management Program, University of St. Gallen, and Tinna C. Nielsen, Founder of Move The Elephant For Inclusiveness.

Why

It can be difficult to see how biases affect us and difficult to be consciously aware of the unconscious in a situation of interaction.

The Inclusion Nudge

Ask reversed questions silently such as *"Would my response to that question/situation/performance/behaviour have been the same if she had been a he?"* or "If he was not 25-years-old but had 25 years more experience than me, would I have listened differently?".

The purpose of the reversed questions are to create emotional triggers when realising our own biased thinking, which can help us change our unconscious thought processes in the moment.

How

- In appraisal interviews or salary negotiations, for example, encourage people to ask themselves,
    - *"Would my response to that question / situation / performance / behaviour have been the same if she had been a he?"*
    - Encourage people to also ask this of each other in evaluations after interviews or in performance reviews.
- In facilitation training or to get buy-in for implementing anonymous screenings ask,
    - *"How do you react if you don't know the gender of a person you're collaborating with virtually?*
    - *Are you annoyed?*

> ○ *Are you relieved when you find out?*
>
> ○ *Do you listen differently?"*

- Pay attention to your reaction when you meet them face-to-face and use that to be more aware of your biases.

- Encourage people to nudge themselves by not seeking out the information about how people look (by looking for them on social media, for example).

Impact

Such efforts usually lead to a higher level of reflection and to emotional triggers that can contribute to listening more thoughtfully.

INCLUSION NUDGES

Practical Techniques for Behaviour, Culture, & System Change to Mitigate Unconscious Bias &
Create Inclusive Organisations

"FRAMING" Inclusion Nudge:

SEEK OUT TWO POSSIBILITIES ABOUT A PERSON TO COUNTERING AUTOMATIC JUDGMENTS

Submitted by: Vernā Myers, Vernā Myers Consulting Group

Why

In a microsecond, we automatically take in information about people we see and make decisions about them. *"Am I safe or not?"*, *"Who are they?"* and so on. This unreflected reaction in our brains triggers ways we interact with others. We do this even when we are aware of our biases and the impact they may have. We need to look at people through a new frame to catch our impulses.

The Inclusion Nudge

Say to yourself; *"There are at least two possibilities about this person."*

How

When seeing someone you don't know, say to yourself: *"There are at least two possibilities for who this person is."* If you can't think of two possibilities, then don't speak until you can.   Some examples could be:

- You see a petite black woman wearing scrubs in the grocery market. Is she a nurse or a doctor?
- You see a young woman, surrounded by men, at the end of a large conference table. Is she a client or a secretary?
- You see a black man cutting grass in front of a beautiful house in a predominately white neighbourhood. Is he the owner or the landscaper?

Impact

This process helps catch automatic sorting decisions, stereotypes and assumptions. When we have only one story about a person, it can determine bias and behaviours (either positive or negative). By forcing our brains to consider other stories, we are more open to other interpretations, which is critical to inclusive behaviour.

"FRAMING" Inclusion Nudge:

'TALK TO THE PERSON' COSTUMER SERVICE

Submitted by: Stephen Frost, CEO of Frost Included, former Head of Diversity & Inclusion at The London Organising Committee of the Olympic and Paralympic Games (LOCOG)

Why

In general there is a tendency that people talk to the carer/assistant of a person with a disability instead of to the person. It was important to create another culture and behaviour to make sure people with disabilities experience more respect and better customer service (in face to face situations). During the Olympic Games and especially during the Paralympic Games this was a great focus. And it was of high priority that all people felt included and that the 220.000 people working at the Games were able to be themselves (not insecure when interacting with people with a disability) and as a result personalise the customer connection.

The Inclusion Nudge

'Talk to the person' in customer service. Reframe 'customer' to 'person' and 'disabled' to 'person'. Illustrate with a short theatre play ("FEEL THE NEED" Inclusion Nudge) what it feels like to not be seen or spoken with, but the carer/assistant/mother/pet next to you is being asked to answer or make decisions on your behalf.

After this motivational eye-opener make a short statement about what it takes to change this and give good customer service: 'Talk to the person'! Make it a mantra.

This contributes to creating a perception of customers as a person to interact with and not an 'object' to deal with (through the carer/assistant). It contributed to reframing the perception of a person with disability.

How

Preparing for the London Olympic Games and the Paralympic Games of 2012, the LOCOG arranged sessions for 1000 employees/volunteers at a time in a stadium, where they played the theatre for them and introduced them to the 'action': Talk to the person. This was stated as often as possible.

Impact

200,000 people at LOCOG were coached to 'talk to the person' and the disability confident attitude of the employees and volunteers resulted in exponentially higher customer feedback scores from disabled people themselves.

Authors' Comments

We believe simple 'reframing' interventions like this are something that all of us can apply more in our work. They are so powerful. Also repeating the reframed or new phrase often helps with the change in perception in yourself and others hearing it.

"FRAMING" Inclusion Nudge:

TWO VERSIONS OF JOB POSTINGS TO SPOTLIGHT LANGUAGE IMPACT

Submitted by: Axel Jentzsch, BASF SE, Diversity + Inclusion

Why

Job postings are generated in a relatively standardized way. The job titles as well as the wording in the postings tend to be influenced by male-dominant language. They stress aspects of hierarchy, power and influence more than aspects of purpose, meaning or creativity. These postings do not appeal to a broad and diverse talent pool which is needed in the company.

The Inclusion Nudge

To get more applications from more diverse applicants, two different versions of jobs were posted in parallel.

How

The two versions were:
- The traditional way
- With changed titles, job descriptions and requirements.

The wording was changed to make it more appealing to individuals from the target group (e.g. women), knowing that even within a given target group there is of course a huge variability.

The purpose is to see if the pools of applicants for the two versions differed. If so, this data can be used to make managers feel the need to change the wording of postings, and understand that their areas of motivation might be different from that of potential applicants.

Impact

Not enough experience yet to evaluate statistically if there is a difference and if this can be used to nudge managers to more inclusive behaviour.

"FRAMING" Inclusion Nudge:

USE PINK TO ALTER UNCONSCIOUS BEHAVIOUR

Submitted by Serio França Leão, Sustainability, Odebrecht

Why

Odebrecht is the largest construction company in Latin America. In the early period of the Santo Antonio Hydropower project there was a focus on increasing numbers of women in the workforce. By mid-2009, approximately 12% of the 10,000 workers at the site were women, many working as operators, electricians, carpenters and drivers. One of the difficulties was getting men to respect that individual toilets at each work site were gender specific. Men would use both.

The Inclusion Nudge

Prime the specific behaviour by using colour. In this case, pink was used on the door of the women's rest room to create the unconscious association to women, thus triggering the behavioural change.

How

Painting toilet doors in different colours: blue for men and pink for women.

Impact

Not surprisingly, men's use of women's toilets dropped nearly to zero. Changing the frame by using the colour pink sent a fast message to the unconscious brain and altered behaviour, leading to respect for women's privacy (thus a more inclusive workplace).

"FRAMING" Inclusion Nudge:

INCLUSIVE LANGUAGE

Submitted by Mag. Virginia Argarate, Menschen Lesen Menschen, D & I
Management

Why

The organisation Virginia was working with decided to intensify its Diversity and
Anti-oppressive practice. Written and verbal communication should be inclusive
of all groups within the agency and community. It was a very sensitive theme
since the organisation serves families and children in critical life situations. The
challenge is to create and implement a language about various groups of people
(i.e. ethnicity, disability etc.) and a language to challenge assumptions about
people and groups of people.

The Inclusion Nudge

Display the language of inclusion, the words and questions in as many places as
possible, prodding not only staff but also clients to apply these words when
engaging in sensitive topics without fear of saying the wrong thing. The nudge
for inclusiveness was to show the way without telling people what to do.

How

- Build and maintain a brief glossary of words and expressions for inclusive
communication with co-workers and clients.
- Involve everyone in developing a glossary of inclusive language to ensure
ownership from the beginning.
- In a training day for the whole agency, everyone brainstormed about
minorities, exclusion, names for these minorities (proper and improper
names) and issues related to these topics. They listed all the expressions on
a board. It was a long list. It was not clear if some words were offensive or
not.
- Participants all agreed that it was hard to find the right words when
assertiveness was needed to achieve empathy. It became clear that what
was right for one social worker wasn't right for others. There was a lack of
knowledge that was impairing not only their approach to the clients, but
their internal relationships as an organisation of diverse people. They agreed

on the need and convenience of one tool and a simple approach to help create more inclusive communication. These were the steps:

- o They chose six terms where they felt unsure: ableism vs. handicap (mental health included), sexual identity, racism/ethnocentrism, sexism/heterosexism and classism.
- o They agreed to deal with one "ism" per month.
- o The whole agency (including front doors, the lobby, conference rooms, offices, toilets and corners in the smoking and eating areas, parking lot, even the website) was colourfully decorated with stickers, each featuring one word or polite question and the invitation to "add your own".
- o Develop cultural competence: knowing how to ask questions in a respectful way.

- Each employee received via e-mail a monthly *"ism* glossary" containing words and expressions considered proper for minorities.

Impact

The Canadian ONG that Virginia worked with has been using this Inclusion Nudge for the past eight years to train its workers to incorporate the glossary. It is not a manual, but includes words and expressions that stick in their minds. This nudge affected the way co-workers speak to each other and how they address issues with clients in an inclusive way. The nudge increased personal comfort to ask "those questions".

© T. Nielsen & L. Kepinski, 2016
www.inclusion-nudges.org

"FRAMING" Inclusion Nudge:
PICTURES TO COUNTER STEREOTYPES

Submitted by: Ursula A. Wynhoven, General Counsel, United Nations Global
Compact

Why

Tests and research on leadership show that the majority of people implicitly
associate caretakers and women, regardless of what we know about men being
caretakers or having traits associated with "softer values". Changing the gender-
specific association of caretaker will have crucial impact on unconscious
perceptions of women as competent leaders and thus on women's career
opportunities and salary levels.

The Inclusion Nudge

The above picture of a walking path in Helsinki (taken by Ursula A. Wynhoven when she visited Finland in 2014) and the two others (taken by Lisa Kepinski in Denmark in 2014) are signs outside men's and women's toilets in a workplace. They are examples of how to change the implicit association of women=caretaker by framing caretaker with the male gender. The Inclusion Nudge is to prime a specific association in the unconscious brain: man=caretaker.

How

Display images of men as caretakers in strategically important places in your organisation, including postings of leadership positions, meeting rooms and internal communication.

Find the inspiration to display "nurturing leadership skills" in research done over the past 30 years on the leadership competencies rated most important to overall leadership effectiveness[41]. Women are stereotypically associated with nurturing competencies such as developing others, building relationships, exhibiting integrity, engaging in self-development, collaboration and motivation. This is a problem since research (see reference above) shows that more women are rated as better overall leaders (12 out of 16 competencies) than men, including competencies that are typically associated with male leaders such as taking initiative, championing change and driving for results.

Authors' Comments

We created this Inclusion Nudge based on Ursula's submitted picture and purpose. We have added a photo. This nudge is not from an organisation, but from a society. We find it relevant as internal inspiration, and have included it in this Guidebook. What images in your workplaces reinforce implicit associations, stereotypes, and biases?   Challenge your own and others' unreflected perceptions with pictures/images that counter these. Share your photos with us via the book's website www.Inclusion-Nudges.org   and we'll publish in an upcoming newsletter.

"FRAMING" Inclusion Nudges

SECTION SUMMARY

Keep in mind that the purpose of "FRAMING" Inclusion Nudges is to alter perceptions to help the brain to perceive issues related to inclusion, diversity, equality in a resource discourse, and to prime specific associations. This helps to promote inclusive behaviours by altering the frame or change the anchor of the thought process.

See Section 7 for information on designing "FRAMING" Inclusion Nudges.

Section 6: OTHER BEHAVIOURAL ECONOMIC INTERVENTIONS SUPPORTING DEVELOPMENT OF INCLUSIVE ORGANISATIONS

Getting a large number of people to execute and implement the I&D initiatives and priorities that have been agreed to, is a struggle in most organisations. Here are some other behavioural economic interventions you can apply. These are generic and can be used to get movement, commitment, compliance, and accountability in I&D work and any other kind of organisational change process.

Compliance and Accountability: Follow the Herd and Reverse the Business Case

Compliance and accountability are often linked to legislation or financial incentives (for example, leaders not getting their bonus if they don't reach their diversity targets). We believe that behavioural insights on motivation must be applied to I&D work. Research shows that external targets and reward incentives do not sufficiently motivate this behaviour[42].

What to Do:

Show the Behaviour of the Herd:

A simple, powerful trick to get compliance is to show what other colleagues, units or companies are doing (only, of course, when their behaviour is what we are aiming for). The more similar they are, the more powerful the pull. When communicating on an intranet or when reporting, simply add such information as "Eight out of 10 departments in your business unit are doing...." or "7 out of 10 of your colleagues have completed the I&D learning sessions and two-thirds of them see performance improvements" or "10 out of 12 of our leadership teams have already reach the target on…". Behavioural economics provide plenty of evidence that humans constantly look to the herd, meaning the majority, the social norm, and those doing better than ourselves, for cues about how to behave. Sometimes the social cues for what is "good" to do are hidden, which is why we as change agents need to publicize the social norm.

Reverse the Business Case:

As organisational change agents we are often asked to present a business case. A traditional business case shows what we gain when the organisation changes. As behavioural studies illustrate, it is often more effective to show what the organisation or person stands to lose by *not* changing, as well as how the proposal/case is not only beneficial but also unique. Since we are twice as miserable (emotional) about what we lose as we are gaining the exact same, commitment and compliance to I&D related policies or process changes might also be more likely to occur and materialise into reality when people are presented with a reversed business case.

Learning and Development: Automatic Enrolment as the Default

Training, learning and capability-building activities on I&D, Unconscious Bias (UB), Cultural Intelligence (CI) are either mandatory or not. If they are mandatory, some people participate only because they have been told to – leaving little room for actual learning. When they are not mandatory, it can be difficult to get people to participate, not necessarily because they are hostile to the idea but sometimes just because they don't get around to signing up. We also see that when people go on international assignments many of them fail to get cultural competency training even though the organisation has implemented such a program. The business case is clear in these situations: the success rate is higher for employees who are culturally competent and when their (expatriates) family have completed cultural competency training. When international assignments are not a success, it is often due to cultural aspects, or to the family not integrating well in the new cultural context. We believe we need to help people do what is best for them and the organisation.

What to Do:

Automatic Enrolment:

Enrol people automatically in learning activities (I&D, UB, CI) instead of relying on them to opt in. Send them the date and venue and withdraw the cost from their cost centre. If the activity is not mandatory, people still have the freedom to opt out. This is a behavioural economics trick to help people comply with strategically important requirements that help the organisation as well as the individual. For the human mind it is equally complex to opt out as to opt in, so very few people will chose to opt out of the training.

Make Them Follow the Herd:

Make sure you inform people on a regular basis about what the others are doing right. For example publicly communicate when a majority of similar others (from their Business Group, department, unit, team etc.) have enrolled or completed the training/learning activity. Inform what they are doing right and that they are doing better (only if they are!).

Commitment to Change and Making It Stick: Shrink the Change and Complexity

More and more organisations publicly commit to working on I&D, but that is not the same as having a commitment from the people in the organisation. We don't mean the commitment they say they have. We mean the (unconscious) commitment that is turned into behaviours that promote inclusiveness – in other words, "Walking the Talk" rather than "Talking the Talk".

What to Do:

Shrink the change from small to big commitments:

Concept owners of such organisational processes as recruitment, learning, reward, procurement or innovation must collaborate with I&D experts to ensure inclusiveness. This is critical in promoting systemic and cultural changes that enable organisations to leverage the opportunities that Inclusion & Diversity brings. Change agents for inclusiveness often ask other professionals to change an organisational process that they believe is designed right for the organisation. Using behavioural economics as a guiding principle we can promote commitment and buy-in to changes if we get people to commit to a small change first.

Reminders:

Design some triggers that remind people to do the behaviour continuously. These are useful when people are both motivated and have the ability (it is simple to do).

If you are interested in learning more about this, you can find inspiration in the RSA animated video[43] of the research by Robert Cialdini and Steve Martin (see resource list). We also recommend that you use the framework from SWITCH by the Heath brothers about how to move elephants (System 1) and steer the rider (System 2). They give various examples illustrating this.

By now, you should have enough inspiration to try out some of the Inclusion Nudges in your own organisation. If you want to learn about how to design Inclusion Nudges and apply these techniques systematically in your organisation, read on and get an introduction to the underlying theory and academic research behind the techniques and _how_ to design powerful Inclusion Nudges.

Section 7: DESIGN INCLUSION NUDGES

WHAT CHARACTERISES A POWERFUL INCLUSION NUDGE?

As an Inclusion Nudge designer, you should keep in mind a few simple principles to create interventions that alter people's behaviour towards more inclusiveness. An Inclusion Nudge should be a simple practical intervention that helps people make better decisions (more objective), promotes inclusion, and reduces unconscious bias as an inherent part of doing business as usual.

Four Key Principles for Designing Inclusion Nudges

1. Motivate both the brain's automatic system and its reflected system

Understanding the need for diversity is not enough; people must *feel* the need for change to achieve sustainable behavioural shifts that improve businesses and workplaces. To bring about effective, long-term behavioural changes, we must target the whole brain and motivate its two interdependent systems. However, the two systems call for different methods (see the audit and design process below).

2. Target specific behavioural drivers

Understanding human motivation and behaviour is key to designing Inclusion Nudges that will promote more inclusive actions and sustainable behavioural changes. These behavioural drivers and fallibilities of the mind can be turned into powerful Inclusion Nudges. When designing Inclusion Nudges (all behavioural interventions) it requires an in-depth audit of motivation, perception, context, hidden barriers, and constraints in order to target the 'right' behavioural drivers (see the audit and design process and List 1 below for how to make these).

3. Do not forbid or punish

An Inclusion Nudge should be non-intrusive, meaning that the behavioural change should not be motivated by punishment or financial incentive. A nudge has the purpose of laying out alternative choices. Designers of Inclusion Nudges should lay out alternative options that lead to behavioural changes that will make inclusiveness stick in the long run.

4. Keep it simple

To motivate the automatic subconscious, we need to "shrink" the change. People are more likely to accept change if it is simple. This can be done by making the Inclusion Nudge an integrated part of existing organisational processes, a simple practical intervention — not something that is extra or that people have to actively think about.

DESIGNING INCLUSION NUDGES

Having an understanding of inclusive behaviours and the drivers of the unconscious mind is a prerequisite for designing powerful Inclusion Nudges. There are no shortcuts. We know from our own experience that it can be a challenge to design Inclusion Nudges that change cultures; we also know that it can be done with the proper positioning. We often hear people say, "*I don't know how to come up with such simple ideas.*" We have found that Inclusion Nudges (or any nudge, for that matter) are not ideas that simply pop up. They emerge from in-depth knowledge of the challenges for I&D in the organisational culture as well as in the unconscious mind. One of the necessary first steps is to have an understanding of unconscious bias, human motivation, behavioural drivers, and decision-making. Next is having clarity about which issues are being affected by biased decision-making or behaviour. Last comes digging deep, examining where in the process, culture, and employee life cycle are the key choice points.

The Audit & Design Process Step by Step

We find that in a straight forward set of six clear steps that you can begin designing and implementing effective Inclusion Nudges within your organisation. These are described below in more detail, and additional support can be found on this Guidebook's website (www.inclusion-nudges.org), in the Inclusion Nudges Community newsletter, and through engaging with Tinna and Lisa for

© T. Nielsen & L. Kepinski, 2016
www.inclusion-nudges.org

direct coaching and/or bringing an Inclusion Nudges Learning Lab to you and your colleagues (details on the book's website and at the end of this Guidebook).

Audit

1. Identify the challenge & the desired behaviour
2. Identify the current behaviour & hidden barriers
3. Analyse motivation, ability/simplicity, and perception

Design

4. Identify behavioural drivers to target
5. Design the inclusion nudges and other interventions
6. Practice, follow up, measure

Audit

In addition to below, refer to List 1 for much more detailed information.

1. Identify the Challenge & the Desired Behaviour

WHAT are the challenges for creating a more inclusive culture?

Undoubtedly, most I&D practitioners can immediately answer this question with some of their most prevalent challenges. This is not unusual in I&D work, which is essentially about culture change, which inherently brings resistance both from personal and organizational/system levels. Some I&D challenge examples could be:

- Improving how diverse perspectives are applied in task-solving and decision-making
- Increasing the gender-balanced pipeline
- Supporting new ways of working with a flexible model
- Gaining leadership support for a new initiative, reducing homogeneity, and increasing diversity in teams
- ....

(See List 1 below for some more common challenges).

© T. Nielsen & L. Kepinski, 2016
www.inclusion-nudges.org

To go deeper on the I&D challenges, use data from internal surveys, audits, anthropological culture analysis, organisational culture audits, global benchmarks, etc. Some examples of this could be:

- Data reveals limited mix of employee population across various organisational levels, departments, and/or in various company sponsored programs (example, funding and support to attend an external Executive MBA course).
- Listen to the managers' and employees' experiences with established organisational systems and processes (qualitative data). Often this will point to an issue to be investigated further.
- There are many common or very similar processes used by companies, especially related to talent. Benchmark with other organisations on where they have identified potential for bias within their existing systems and processes.

WHAT is the desired behaviour that can address this challenge?

Be as specific as you can be. You might need to describe different behaviours in a sequence.

WHAT kind of behavioural change do you want to facilitate?

Some examples could be: 'new behaviour', 'intensify existing behaviour', and/or 'decrease existing behaviour'. You might have to design interventions of various kinds in the same sequence, such as activating a new behaviour and decreasing an existing behaviour (for example, start leveraging diversity of perspectives and stop seeking out similar people for input) below.

2. Identify the Current Behaviour & Hidden Barriers

WHAT is characterising the behaviour today? *WHAT* does the data (qualitative/quantitative) show?

WHAT are the critical decision points in a change process or perception?

This is a process that we call *"Digging Deep"*. The micro decisions that go unexamined often have a macro impact on the outcome. It is important to analyse what is driving behaviour in a particular situation/context at a particular time to target the right behavioural drivers and influencers.

Dig deep in the data, look for patterns, and ask yourself:

- What patterns do the data show and what patterns do the data not show?
- What decisions have been made previously (the process design)?
- What were the consequences of those decisions on the issue being examined?
- How were those evaluations, information processing, or decisions typically made?
- If these are not the reasons for the status quo, then what are the reasons?
- How does this seemingly neutral process affect different demographic groups?
- How could men and women (and other diverse groups) understand this question or these requirements differently and what could be the consequences?
- What can be tweaked or changed to alter the outcome?
- What kind of perception, mindset, and behaviour is causing the gap/barrier right now?
- How is this team working together – how are group dynamics and team culture affecting them?
- .....

WHAT needs to change among individuals or in systems to reach the intended outcome?

Be persistent in exploring and digging to the core of perceptions, norms, processes, choice points, and decision-making. Eventually, a pattern will emerge that sheds light on why subconscious decisions were made, or at least on trouble spots to be addressed. Inclusion Nudges can encourage different types of behaviour – conscious choices vs. an intuitive response – so it is important to be clear on what issues you are designing for and targeting. Once you get to this point, you are ready to analyse the behavioural drivers to target with the Inclusion Nudges.

3. Analyse Motivation, Ability / Simplicity, & Perception

When people perform a specific behaviour or change behaviour, they often are motivated, have the ability to do it, and it is easy to do. All of these occur at the same time. It is equally important that their perception of inclusion and diversity is (unconsciously) resource-oriented. The following are the focal areas of Inclusion Nudges, and thus need to be analysed.

Motivation:

WHAT is the level of motivation for inclusion & diversity (high or low)?

Some ways that this can show up are:

- **High level of motivation:** People have good intentions for I&D, when they *feel* the need and when they explicitly request change towards inclusion.

- **Low level of motivation:** People are sceptical, cynical, express doubt, see I&D as nice to have, etc.

- **Conflicting levels of motivation:** Be aware in cases where if people stand to lose power or if they are experiencing a feeling of threat, disgust, anger, sadness, pity, or fear, then they might publicly express their personal motivation for change, but in the unconscious mind they might favour the status quo.

These can, of course, vary from person to person, from time to time, and within varying organisational contexts.

INCLUSION NUDGES

Practical Techniques for Behaviour, Culture, & System Change to Mitigate Unconscious Bias &
Create Inclusive Organisations

WHAT ways are the two systems of the brain motivated for inclusion & diversity?

- The reflected "System 2" is motivated when the destination is meaningful (within the context and for the individual), the business case is clear, and when complexity is low. This means that the critical moves towards inclusion are scripted and easy to follow.[44] This is very much linked to ability (see below).

- The automatic "System 1" is motivated for a behavioural change towards inclusion when:
  - *Feelings* have been triggered (such as surprise, excitement, empathy, shame, disgust). If people have had an emotional experience with exclusion of self or others, or have *seen* the implications of non-inclusion, they are likely to have a high motivation to change status quo. If they are part of the privileged group and are blind to their own privileges you can assume they are less likely to be motivated (regardless of stated good intentions).
  - Another core motivator is *primitive responses* such as self-preservation, which is about survival. If people stand to lose privileges and power, and their group of similar others (remember, we unconsciously act like tribe people) are threatened, then assume people are less motivated to act inclusive (regardless of rational intentions to be inclusive). Social acceptance/rejection dominates most of our behaviour. If other colleagues are not showing inclusive behaviour or no role models are visible, then people who deviate from the social norm by taking the lead on inclusion & diversity are less likely to be motivated (regardless of their rational good intentions).
  - *Anticipation of the outcome* (for example: gain/loss or hope/fear) of being inclusive/exclusive is also a strong motivator. The hope of something good coming from inclusion is strong, but often the fear of loss (such as talent or performance) can be a high

motivator for inclusion, as loss aversion is a strong behavioural influencer. Another way this dynamic can show up is if people have had bad experiences with diversity, the fear of failure, will often prevent them from acting inclusive.

"FEEL THE NEED" Inclusion Nudges focuses on increasing motivation, but if motivation is already high in both systems of the brain, there is no need to design this kind of motivational Inclusion Nudge. Then, look to begin work on the other elements and types of Inclusion Nudges to turn motivation into behavioural change.

When designing Inclusion Nudges or any other kind of behavioural intervention that aims to change people's behaviour, it is absolutely key that we have insights into the level of motivation and in what ways people are motivated. Otherwise, we will be left guessing which will increase the risk of the intervention not working.

Ability/Simplicity:

Ability is not only about having the skills, mindset, or enablers to perform in an inclusive manner. It is also about simplicity. *How simple and easy is it to do the behaviour without having to use willpower and reflection (energy)?*
So, when analysing the level of ability and simplicity, you have to look at:

- Does it require a lot of conscious thought processing?
- Does it require a lot of physical effort?
- Is it non-routine?
- Does it take more time?
- Does it cost more money?
- Is it going against the social norm?

If the answers to these questions are *"yes"*, then it is not easy (low ability) to change behaviour regardless of good intentions.

"PROCESS" Inclusion Nudges focuses on increasing ability to perform inclusive behaviour by making it easy to do for the individual. If ability is already high, assess whether motivation needs to be increased or perception altered. Perhaps you need to consider one of the more general behavioural interventions to make sure the inclusive behaviour will be sustained.

Perception:

WHAT are the underlying perceptions of inclusion, diversity, equality, and related issues?

To make sure these perceptions support inclusive behaviour and the behavioural change you aim for with your intervention, is it important to analyse these perceptions and what shapes them.

Images and words have connotations and trigger unconscious associations. In the case of language, words construct the social world, its reality and meaning. Words and the way information is presented are anchors in our thought processes. Words prime our reactions and behaviours in a specific direction. Images, words, context, setting, and questions function as a frame for how we perceive issues. Diversity, gender equality, inclusion, and similar issues are often dominated by a discourse of moral and social responsibility that often results in 'nice-to-have' attitudes towards inclusion. When that is the case, it is difficult to achieve true inclusion where diversity is leveraged for performance and innovation. It is important to analyse the dominant discourse.

WHAT have been the patterns in information/focus about I&D in your organisation so far?

- Has the focus been on minorities and women?
- Has only minority data been presented? What kind of information is presented first and last?
- Is the focus only on the challenges of diversity and/or the successful examples?
- Have all questions that are being asked in processes been tested to see if these are perceived equally by a diverse group? (For example in the talent management process, competencies used in job adverts, or when asking about international mobility.)

© T. Nielsen & L. Kepinski, 2016
www.inclusion-nudges.org

"FRAMING" Inclusion Nudges focus on creating perceptions with associations to diversity as a resource and inclusion as an enabler to performance and innovation by changing the frame or anchor of the thought process. This type of Inclusion Nudge also aims to change connotations and associations inherent in organisational processes and the unconscious mind of people. For example by framing a seemingly neutral question differently the question will be perceived differently and thus how people answer it, creating other opportunities for the individual. By framing the competency requirements differently, a more diverse group of qualified people might apply.

! Watch out for biases that may creep into the barrier-seeking process (this is where it can be very helpful to have an external, neutral partner to conduct an organisational scan for biases and ask questions for reflection). This knowledge provides the foundation for designing powerful Inclusion Nudges. Since an Inclusion Nudge is a simple intervention it often comes across as an idea that just popped up, but that is rarely the case. Most Inclusion Nudges are designed based on a profound analytical process of digging deep for the root cause of status quo.

Design

4. Identify Behavioural Drivers to Target

Since human behaviour is driven primarily by the unconscious mind that operates on short cuts and automatic processes, called cognitive biases, we have to design the behavioural interventions to target these. Cognitive biases can be both barriers to inclusive behaviour, but also levers to behavioural change. In the audit phase, we have identified barriers to target. The next step is to identify which of the behavioural drivers to target and turn into levers for behavioural change. Research has identified more than 150 cognitive biases[45]. For Inclusion Nudges, some of those that are the most important (from what we have identified until now) are listed below:

Subjective Choice

Overconfidence

Confirmation Bias

Status Quo Bias

Loss Aversion

In-Group & Out-Group

Follow the Herd (Conformity)

Framing

Anchor

Recency Effect

Priming

Default

See List 1 for a description of each of these behavioural drivers (biases and heuristics), insight in how they affect individuals and workplaces, and some ways on how to target these and transform them from being barriers for inclusion to being levers for inclusion.

5. Design Inclusion Nudges and Other Interventions

Based on the information gathered, design Inclusion Nudges that trigger the mind toward inclusive behaviour. Use the four key designing principles: tap into the whole brain; focus on the behavioural drivers; do not force the choice through coercion; keep it simple.

Once you have identified which of the three types on Inclusion Nudges you need to design and how many (you might need more of one type or perhaps all three types), you need to prioritise them in order to facilitate and implement them to have the biggest impact. To do this is can be an advantage to map the decision/behaviour process.

! Remember that you are focusing on a *subconscious cognitive process,* not a *conscious good practice*. Although Inclusion Nudges may be embedded in good practices, the focus of Inclusion Nudges is on automatic, quick thinking. See the examples later in this section on the distinction between good practices and Inclusion Nudges for more understanding on this aspect.

6. Practice, Follow up, Measure

Experiment with this process. Adjust as needed. Measure the result (if the intervention is successful, then use it to 'motivate the herd'). Be aware that the most powerful Inclusion Nudges often come from experimentation. You might need to target different behavioural drivers or biases than you targeted the first time, or you might need to design more Inclusion Nudges to support the first interventions. You might also have to design some 'reminder' triggers that are useful when people are both motivated and have the ability (it is simple to do). This can be as simple as a text message, a poster, an email, a sound, displayed words, etc.

Organisations that have already implemented unconscious-bias awareness will have an advantage in spreading the practice of designing Inclusion Nudges; however, don't worry if your organisation is not yet at this point. To start, you need a core group of people who are key process owners or decision makers; they should have a foundational understanding of inclusion, behavioural drivers, and unconscious bias. As unconscious bias awareness is shared more widely in your organisation, more and more people will be ready to join the core team and start designing Inclusion Nudges. By sharing your successes internally you will tap into the "Follow the Herd" dynamic, and thus, get more people engaged in the process.

LIST 1: COGNITIVE BIASES & HOW TO TARGET THESE WITH INCLUSION NUDGES

Organisations are created and designed by humans. As a result, their structure and processes are embedded with human patterns of thinking, decision-making and bias. Most organisations, regardless of industry or sector, have internal challenges and implicit barriers as part of their culture, history and structure. Often these are perceived as unchangeable and part of the core culture (*"that's always the way it's been done around here"* or *"it defines our culture; it makes us who we are"*), and the culture is often "invisible" to the people because they "just do" the culture un-reflected as part of their daily actions in the organisational settings they are in. The culture also "dictates" a specific way you have to look, behave, talk, interact etc. to be accepted as a part of the group and to be perceived as competent and trustworthy. These implicit norms favour some people over others and result in various degrees of exclusion and inclusion, through the organisational processes, structures, culture, collaboration, and leadership.

For the culture-change practitioner, there are some specific biases and human behavioural drivers that will affect how you succeed in getting buy-in or commitment to systemic and behavioural changes or implementation of initiatives, how you will be able to communicate the need for behavioural changes, and how you can motivate for this.

Below are some of the behavioural drivers to target with Inclusion Nudges. You often need to target several of these with various Inclusion Nudges.

Subjective Choice	Follow the Herd (Conformity)
Overconfidence	Framing
Confirmation Bias	Anchor
Status Quo Bias	Recency Effect
Loss Aversion	Priming
In-Group & Out-Group	

Subjective Choice

What is it?

Most evaluations of people and decision-making are unconscious and subjective (though we believe they can be made objective and rational). Due to this process in the automatic system of the brain, we will have a positive association toward people who are like us or with whom we have had positive experiences, as well as with those who fit the organisation's norms.

Some ways it can show up in the workplace

- Assessing and interviewing candidates or employees for organisational "fit".

- Tendency to network with the likeable and similar over the competent.

- Giving some clients over others a better treatment / solution.

- Selecting staff for projects.

- Giving informal helpful development feedback to some people and not to others.

What to do

Unconscious bias awareness is critical but not sufficient. We can help design choice processes to be more objective and to shift the mode of thinking ("PROCESS" Inclusion Nudges). We can illustrate to people their behavioural patterns to help them see their patterns ("seeing is believing"), and the implications of these. We can guide choices by triggering emotions such as surprise, loss, disappointment or hope ("FEEL THE NEED" Inclusion Nudges). We can shift the implicit norm for 'the ideal leader/employee' ("FRAMING" Inclusion Nudges).

© T. Nielsen & L. Kepinski, 2016
www.inclusion-nudges.org

Overconfidence

What is it?

A strong tendency to be overly optimistic about a choice or evaluation (of a person or information). Overconfidence Bias can also show up with In-Group Bias, where we trust the opinions of people in our In-Group more than those of the Out-Group.

Some ways it can show up in the workplace

- In hiring decisions, where there is a prevailing belief that *"we only hire the best"*, decisions are often very subjective by overlooking alternative candidates from a set belief of what *"the best"* looks like (for example, only from some universities or some other companies in their work experience). Furthermore, these subjective decisions are often flawed with biased thinking, such as with Selective Attention Bias (we see what we are looking for and overlook what we are not looking for) and Confirmation Bias (focusing on data that confirms our decision).

- In performance reviews a manager soliciting feedback on an employee may place greater weight on feedback from people in the In-Group.

- Overconfidence in one's ability to be objective, fair, and inclusive.

- Believing that the data show an objective reality (thus not exploring what the data is not showing).

What to do

We can illustrate the consequences of choices that reflect the organisational culture, challenging the overconfident belief that we are making an objective choice. Rather than convince, we must show the results of a choice that counters the assumption that something is a success or failure. We can spot patterns of behaviour in data that counter the bias conviction and design interventions that reveal these patterns ("FEEL THE NEED" Inclusion Nudges). We can design process interrupters that force the brain to see the counter facts in a new perspective (bias is relative) ("PROCESS" and "FRAMING" Inclusion Nudges).

© T. Nielsen & L. Kepinski, 2016
www.inclusion-nudges.org

Confirmation Bias

What is it?

We search, interpret and remember information in a way that confirms our preconceptions. We say, *"I knew I was right all along"* when in fact we most likely sought out and/or paid attention to information that proved our preconception was right, while ignoring contrary information. Our brain gather data and opinions to confirm[46] what they believe in the first place, making their decisions seem "rational". We display this bias by gathering or remembering information selectively, or by interpreting it in a biased manner. The effect is stronger with emotionally charged issues, as is often the case for I&D. Examples include "belief perseverance" (when beliefs persist after the evidence supporting them is shown to be false), the "irrational primacy effect" (a greater reliance on information encountered early in a series) and "illusory correlation" (when people falsely perceive an association between two events, situations, people).

Some ways it can show up in the workplace

- In interviews, we may believe that a candidate coming from a high-profile company is more qualified than another candidate coming from a lesser-known company, and the hiring decision is swayed based on preconceptions that the *"high-profile company candidate is the BEST candidate"*. All listening and fact gathering is filtered through this preconception and results in only confirming the view, despite having input that the other candidate is very well-qualified.

- Also may show up in performance evaluations and talent discussions, for example if an employee was at one point labelled as a "high potential", then the new managers at later points in time continue this perception by seeking out evidence to support this label versus looking afresh and assessing against a new field of candidates. The same is the case for poor performers.

 © T. Nielsen & L. Kepinski, 2016
www.inclusion-nudges.org

- This bias results in self-fulfilling prophesies because when we believe other people have potential or are great performers, we treat them as such and they are more likely to become that, whereas people who we don't believe in, we treat accordingly and thus they perform poorly. In this way our mind is very powerful in materialising biased beliefs into reality.

What to do

Provide facts or results that counter the rational beliefs and stereotypes (seeing is believing). Show information and showcase people that counter the common perception

Status Quo Bias[47]

What is it?

Change is difficult because people tend to stick with the current situation. They have a cognitive bias for the status quo, which is a point of reference. Any deviation is psychologically perceived as a loss. When complexity in a choice process is high, people tend to retreat to their default behaviour or choice.

Some ways it can show up in the workplace

- Resistance to change (*"that's the way it's always been done around here"*).
- Being blind to the need for new skills and not future-fit.
- Not utilizing the new range to talents as a company globalises more (majority of opportunities go to the headquarters' nationality employees rather than widely distributed across all deserving employees in all countries where the firm operates).
- Hiring a person looking and behaving like the others in the team/or the person previously in the position.
- Not-Invented-Here bias (Practice leads not applying the input given by other specialists)
- A tendency to not recognise the seriousness of unacceptable behaviour such as bullying, harassment, discrimination and the negative influence on all people in the organisation, as well as on performance.
- Internal practitioners who are responsible for the design and development of organisational concepts/processes such as the recruitment process, talent management system, leadership programmes, learning & development activities, reward and performance, innovation processes, and all the others, often do not 'see' the biases embedded in the processes. (Research, from 2014, on the internal barriers I&D professionals face in large organisations found that HR concept owners are a significant challenge to succeeding with creating the crucial systemic and cultural changes).

What to do

Shrink the change by changing the system default to make it easy to perform a new behaviour or designing the process to help the brain unconsciously challenge status quo like with the example of blind screenings ("PROCESS" Inclusion Nudges). Illustrate the implications of the status quo instead of convincing about the need for change ("FEEL THE NEED" Inclusion Nudges). By helping people commit to small changes first, you can mitigate the reaction of fear, thus making it easier for them to commit to bigger changes later ("FRAMING" Inclusion Nudges).

Loss Aversion[48]

What is it?

We are twice as miserable about a loss as we are happy about a gain of the same magnitude. This is linked to our willingness to take risks. Decision makers are risk averse: they prefer the sure thing to the gamble. When it comes to diversity, this means taking the risk of selecting someone different from the recognisable norm. Whether people perceive something as a loss or a gain depends on how the issue is framed.

Some ways it can show up in the workplace

- Perceiving "diversity" as a problem. Have you heard leaders in your organisation equate diversity to "risk"? For example, "*Let's take a risk on promoting _____*" (often said about women). This bias can lead to seriously strong resistance to I&D work.

What to do

You can mitigate loss aversion by reducing the fear of losing privileges as a result of diversity. You can turn lose-aversion into a catalyst for change; instead of presenting business cases of gains, we can illustrate what is lost through status quo behaviour. For example, illustrate the impact of selective attention, a biased lens, and the opportunities missed by not having diversity and inclusion. Make a reverse business case: instead of gaining 30% better performance, we lose 30% performance by not changing. The loss can also be perceived as bigger if framed more broadly: instead of saying that "90% of university students would select our company as a first choice", say that "25,000 university students (10%) would not choose our company" ("FEEL THE NEED" and "FRAMING" Inclusion Nudges). You can also change the system default of the norm which often position the minority or women being a 'risk', by flipping the norm like the example of successor planning where the norm is 'Everyone is ready now'. By having to argue why a person is not ready instead of why a person should be promoted, can help mitigate the sense of taking a risk ("PROCESS" Inclusion Nudges).

In-Group & Out-Group[49]

What is it?

An in-group is a social unit with which a person identifies psychologically. This can be due to similarities, like communication style, food preference, gender, race, job function, etc. In contrast, an out-group is a social unit with which an individual does not identify. Often people will show preference for the in-group over the out-group. This can be expressed in evaluations, allocation of resources and many other ways. Research show that babies prefer people who treat others well over those who treat others badly; however, the majority of babies (6 months) prefer in-group members even if the latter treat out-group members badly.[50]

Some ways it can show up in the workplace

- Most people do not 'reflect' on the organisational/team culture, thus do not see how people and knowledge diversity is being excluded in solving tasks and making decisions about talent and business.

- Organisational processes and structures are perceived as neutral, fair, and objective to all people (especially by those not experiencing the negative impact of these, but only the advantages), and may be seen with the statements such as, *"Our organisation is a Meritocracy."* or *"We have no biases in our system."*

- The privileged are blind to the advantages of their own gender, nationality, and other majority characteristics.

- The privileged are blind to the unequal opportunities of the unprivileged, in part out of belief that they are better, smarter, harder working, etc. (Self-Serving bias, Illusionary Superiority, Curse of Knowledge Bias, Out-Group Bias)

- A Western-headquartered company may have a leadership competency called *"confidence"* that does not fit Asian males or Indian females who are still seen as having strong leadership skills within their own region. As a result they are consistently overlooked for promotion to headquarters roles due to low ratings on this trait. Leadership roles continue to mirror the founders, resulting in the "Mini-Me Effect".

- Informal networks can arise around information sharing, visibility, key project assignments or promotions. When people are not perceived as part of the in-group their information is not processes as much, or they are not hired or get as much informal feedback or recognition.

- Micro-behaviour will reproduce/sustain in-groups and out-groups and inequality in opportunities. These easily becomes self-fulfilling prophecies.

- Strengthen and sustain silos (functional, markets, categories, units, teams) and mistrust that prevent knowledge sharing in a matrix organisations.

What to do

We can design processes to avoid in-group preferences – for example, by creating other groups that mix similarities and differences to counter an observed preference (i.e. max. 70% of the same nationality, gender, generation in the same team) ("FRAMING" Inclusion Nudges). Or, we can design exercises and eye-openers that showcase how the candidates who were unconsciously evaluated on different characteristics reveal patterns of homogeneity and diversity (compared to the evaluators' own characteristics) ("FEEL THE NEED" Inclusion Nudges). We can design processes that ensure interaction across siloes and groups to break down the psychological barriers and create trust in 'the others' ("PROCESS" Inclusion Nudges).

Follow the Herd (Conformity)

What is it?

Humans are social beings and thus greatly influenced – for better and worse – by the behaviour of others, especially those similar to ourselves. Solomon Asch's[51] experiments show that 37% conform to the opinion of the majority in a group even when they believe it is wrong. This mechanism has also proven to have positive effects on people, such as getting them to use a seatbelt by visually informing them about the social norm, like 9 out of 10 people use the seatbelt when driving a car.

Some ways it can show up in the workplace

- Most people are not aware of how much the implicit norms for the 'ideal' type of employee are dominating their interaction with people and decision-making about new hires, promotions, team staffing, talent development and much more.

- In company cultures with strong traditional hierarchy where the leaders set the example, can lead to others conforming to the leader's decisions and behaviour style (all are socialised by the same norm).

- Also can show up in team work, task-solving processes, workshops, business planning, decision-making processes, where people do not speak up. In this way diversity of perspectives are not leveraged for better performance and innovative collaboration.

What to do

Help people unconsciously feel the need to follow the herd in a positive direction, such as by showcasing what the majority behavioural role models are doing (such as being inclusive, reaching targets, completing training).Use the group dynamic as a positive influencer: Showcase inclusive behaviour of the majority to influence the others to do the same ("FEEL THE NEED" and "FRAMING" Inclusion Nudges). Mitigate the group dynamic by designing the processes and ways of collaborating/facilitating to ensure that individuals do not conform to majority views i.e. in people-calibration activities or business planning ("PROCESS" Inclusion Nudges). Conformity drops by two-thirds when an individual responds in private (writing on a note), and only 5% conform when they have an ally or partner (share in smaller groups).

Framing

What is it?

How an issue is presented – words, images, colours, data, environment, information, phrasing – impacts how it is perceived, and thus determines our behaviour and decisions.

Some ways it can show up in the workplace

- A bias can depend on *who* presents an issue. For example, presentations may be received differently when made by junior or senior staff members, by employees from headquarters or the field, by men or women.

- The word diversity often has connotations to minority, a group of people "we need to help", and is often dominated (unconsciously) by a moral rationality more than a business rationale, which can limit our ability to leverage diversity as a resource that can have sustainable impact on business results.

- Diversity targets often focus on minorities, making diversity a 'minority issue' and thus we miss the chance to engage the majority and work as a "whole system" on inclusion.

- The word gender more often has associations with women, which leaves out men and a focus on their inclusion challenge, such as men having the ability to work part time, men being the primary child carer, or elder carer, or learning more about their own culture of masculinity and its upsides and downsides just like any other culture dynamic that I&D programs may focus on.

What to do

Change how we set targets for diversity: focus on majority instead of minority, humanise the numbers, show pictures of people, change percentages into numbers of people. Choose consciously who is presenting – empower business leader to make the intervention/presentation. See the examples of "FRAMING" Inclusion Nudges about shifting associations by shifting the numbers presented.

Don't assume that everyone sees, interprets, or has the same meaning attached to seemingly neutral words, symbols, behaviours, and processes. Check in for the other's understanding. Ensure that the intended meaning can be clearly grasped by all.

Anchor

What is it?

The starting point of a thought process is dominated by the first information given, the words, the questions, what we have seen in the past, or previously had success with. It matters greatly whether a choice is presented as a 9% risk or a 91% opportunity.

Some ways it can show up in the workplace

- With phrases like, *"We've tried that before and it doesn't work"* or *"That's not how we do things around here"*.

- Words can also anchor biases: for example, labelling majority employees *"top talents"* while labelling minority employees *"diverse top talents"*, or having an organisational *"mentoring program"* and a *"women's mentoring program"*. These separate anchors raise the perception that the employees in the diverse programs are *"different"* (read: less qualified) than the *"normal"* (majority) employees in the main programs.

- Seemingly neutral questions like 'Are you internationally mobile?' are non-inclusive because men and women perceive this question differently, thus answer it differently, which results in different career opportunities.

- Many job adverts contain a long list of competency requirements, and this result in a risk of qualified candidates not applying. Research show that women apply when mastering 100% of the competencies, men when mastering 80%.

- Many job adverts are dominated by a masculine dominated language. Since words appeal differently to different people (also based on culture, gender,

INCLUSION NUDGES

Practical Techniques for Behaviour, Culture, & System Change to Mitigate Unconscious Bias &
Create Inclusive Organisations

personality types and more) this limit diversity in the pool
of applicants.

- The order of which candidates/employees are evaluated
matters, because the whether the candidate before the
one being evaluated was rated a poor or high performer
affects the next in line.

What to do

Change the anchor by changing how we ask questions, or
present an issue, by using more nuances in the language we
use to describe competencies and reduce the amount of
competencies listed. See the examples of "FRAMING" Inclusion
Nudges on how to change people's behaviour without relying
on reflection, such as little interventions like present each
evaluator with the candidates in different orders. Show the
implications of the anchor we create without having the
intentions by designing interventions that motivate to change
this. See examples of "FEEL THE NEED" Inclusion Nudges on
how. Implement these Inclusion Nudges in the existing
processes as the calibration and recruitment process etc.

© T. Nielsen & L. Kepinski, 2016
www.inclusion-nudges.org

Recency Effect

What is it?

Information and interactions that occur at the end of an event are recalled more clearly than what was said or done earlier; these become the "anchor" or "frame" for how a person or event is recalled.

Some ways it can show up in the workplace

- Performance assessments and feedback discussions that should encompass a full year (or six months) but actually refer only to the past couple of month's work. Recent performance is rated as having higher value. This especially affects employees in job transitions, or those who have been on leave of absence (given that more women than men take parental leave, this has more negative implications for women).

- Hiring interviews where primarily the closing topics and conversation determine how a candidate's qualifications are judged.

What to do

Set up check-in milestones during a process to record events/information. Don't rely on memory, as the recall will usually not be comprehensive ("PROCESS" Inclusion Nudges). Pro-actively search for and present facts about performance or examples of behaviour that give a holistic view of the person/situation ("FEEL THE NEED" Inclusion Nudges).

Priming

What is it?

An implicit memory effect in which exposure to one stimulus (word, colour, image, temperature, stereotype, positioning) influences a response to another stimulus. Priming can be perceptual, conceptual or visual. Many examples of this exist in our everyday lives. Colours like pink and green have a calming effect. Making words visible has been proven to affect behaviour and influence performance. Holding something cold or warm in your hand can affect feelings towards people. Lines on the road can make people slow down. Bright red and blue text can make people believe more in the information that when it is grey. Also, seen with normative cultures in an organisation or functional area can shape the filter through which we unconsciously evaluate people's style, performance, appearance, etc.

Some ways it can show up in the workplace

- Asking for demographic identity data (gender or age) at the beginning of a skills test or job application affect how people answer the test questions.

- Job titles/positions have gender stereotypical connotations.

- What we see is what we believe, i.e. when we see the majority of leaders being men we unconsciously believe men are more competent leaders. In most organisations the norm for leaders and societies is masculine. Also called "Global Mr Corporate Masculinity", this norm has been identified across Asia, Europe and North America[52].

- Announcing a promotion or introducing a new hire with internal messages that use awkward language about a person's skills, potential, or how they got the role. Or 'New female CEO' is priming the brain to 'see' women as an 'unusual choice'.

- Positively acknowledging some questions or input in a meeting (example: *"That's an important and insightful question, John."*) but not others, prime the brain to see that information as more important and thus process it more than other information.

- Describing work-life or flex work as being a *"working mothers' issue"* makes it a women's issue not a business issue.

What to do

Visually display specific words, images and terms in workplaces that are associative to inclusive behaviour, and to prime specific self-perceptions. Use specific colours to guide perceptions and behaviour. See examples of "FRAMING" Inclusion Nudges.

Default

What is it?

We go with the flow of pre-set options, such as in a system. It matters for the choice process whether the default is to opt-in or opt-out. We see this in organ donation. When asking people to register in the system (opt in) far less than the number of people who have the intention of doing so will register, whereas setting the default as all people registered as organ donors and asking people to opt out of the system will create the result of people acting in accordance with their intentions. We also go with the flow of the pre-set norms in an organisation, i.e. all positions have to be 100% full-time rather than worked flexibly or part-time.

Some ways it can show up in the workplace

We also go with the flow of the pre-set norms in an organization. For example, when we see that all positions in a company are considered as full-time rather than all considered as able to be worked flexibly or part-time as the default position. We see this with the expectation that the Inclusion & Diversity business case must be stated, and often re-stated over and over, such that the subtext default opening position on I&D is always *"prove it is valuable"* or *"justify why"*. In one "FRAMING" Inclusion Nudge example that is in this Guidebook, Alberto Platz has changed the default of the I&D discussions to be "Inclusion & Diversity: Why not?", thus changing the starting point of the discussion. In this case, others must present the arguments _against_ a focus on I&D...not something that many would actually do.

What to do

- Set the system default to automatic enrolment for learning activities, such as for cultural competency trainings for expats and their families or for I&D sessions rolled out across the organization. By starting with a default of all opted in from the beginning, the result is more may actually receive the learning sessions than by relying on them to opt in. For the human mind it is equally complex to opt out as to opt in, so very few people will chose to opt out.

- Another example can be seen with Flex Work by changing the organisational norms (which often may be excluding groups of people and individuals) by changing the default. For example, by stating that all roles can be managed at 80% time instead of 100% time (full-time).   Then, asking managers to argue why not (opt out) instead of arguing why that should be possible (opt in).

- A third example is seen with an Inclusion Nudge shared by Sue Johnson where her organization changed the default in their successor planning from 'who is ready' to 'all are ready now' which forces managers to argue 'why not' (opt out).

YOUR COMMENTS: Join the Discussion

Many more behavioural drivers impact the workplace and should be considered when designing Inclusion Nudges. There are also multiple ways these can show up in the workplace and be dealt with. Visit www.Inclusion-Nudges.org to learn more and to share your examples with us via email. We welcome your insights and will share them across the Global Inclusion Nudges Community via our newsletter, the website, and perhaps in the next edition of the Inclusion Nudges Guidebook.

I&D Good Practices vs. Inclusion Nudges

While requesting examples of Inclusion Nudges, we received many submissions that are good I&D practices, but did *not* apply the behavioural economic techniques. As a reminder, Inclusion Nudges are micro-interventions that target the automatic system of the brain rather than an I&D program or initiative, or rational arguments or information campaigns.

While the collection of I&D Good Practice can be very useful for practitioners, it was not the remit of this project. However, to help further learning for across the Inclusion Nudges Community, we have selected a few of these good I&D practices to illustrate the difference between a practice and an Inclusion Nudge, as well as to illustrate how an Inclusion Nudge can be designed to support implementation of a good practice, get buy-in or make the practice more powerful in terms of commitment, behavioural change, and improve decision-making.

We thank everyone who submitted good practices, and we hope through this Guidebook and its website, that the distinction will become clearer.

Good Practice:

LANGUAGE INCLUSION

Submitted by: Karin Middelburg van Goinga, company anonymous

Why

In a department with more than four nationalities, Karin saw that the language still spoken most often was that of the company headquarters (in this case, Danish). Formal meetings were held in English, but informally people would switch back to Danish. This would exclude some non-Danish speakers and limit the sharing of important information.

The Good Practice

Language posters were placed around the workplace and in meeting rooms to remind people to be language-inclusive by speaking English.

How

- Set the Context: Gather the whole department for a diversity session and paint the picture of how we are all different. For example, Karin asks people to stand up when they can answer yes to questions like: *"Who is under 50 years of age? Who is an engineer? Who has travelled to more than five countries? Who lives in the city?"*
- Link Language to Inclusion: After that, Karin showed why the company considered I&D important. It was agreed that for the sake of inclusion and information sharing, all conversations involving a non-Danish speaker would be held in English. This included social as well as work related discussions. When people did not speak English in mixed-language settings, others had "permission" to ask them to switch to English.
- Gain Commitment: The participants discussed one-on-one what they thought of this approach and how it would affect their everyday office life. This was shared with the larger group.
- Note that this is not a formal policy, nor a requirement for compliance. Employees are still free to choose their use of languages in informal meetings and social gatherings.

Impact

In the weeks after the session, we hung new language posters on the walls as reminders of the language switch. New employees, as well as visitors to the department, were informed of this practice.

Authors' Comments: From Good Practice to Inclusion Nudge

Although this is more of a Good Practice, reminding people of an intention, it is a great example of inclusion. Designing Inclusion Nudges can support this good practice.

For example:

"FEEL THE NEED" Inclusion Nudge:

Appeal to feelings to motivate the change and not solely rational understanding or good intentions because else the automatic system in the brain (the elephant) has to use will power to change the behaviour which is proven to drain us from energy making us under-perform on work tasks. In the initial diversity session you can make interactive exercises making people experience how it feels to be excluded from the conversation.

"FRAMING" Inclusion Nudge:

Prime the brain to act correctly to the good intentions by designing the poster statements as, *"3 out of 10 colleagues of yours speak Danish. What are you and [org.name] missing out on when speaking Danish?"* or keep momentum when the majority is doing the right behaviour; *"7 out of 10 of your colleagues speak our corporate language in meetings and social settings."*

Or shift the mode of thinking from automatic to more reflected; *"Can everyone understand the language you are using now?"*

Good Practice:

NEW HIRE ENGAGEMENT AND A VIEW ON ORGANISATIONAL CULTURE

Submitted by: Flora Marriott, company anonymous

Why

When integrating/on-boarding large numbers of new employees, ensure that they are engaged and productive as soon as possible.

The Good Practice

Send batches of 12 to 20 new starts into the offices for an hour with the mission of sitting with existing employees and asking them: *"What is it like to work here? What's great? What's not so good?"*

How

I wanted new employees to feel and breathe the culture from day one. Many on-boarding programmes "tell" new starts about the culture and values of the company they've joined. But there can be a mismatch between espoused values and lived values and behaviour.

When the new starts returned to the training room with their findings, we would discuss what they had learnt. Obviously, they found out about the negatives as well as the positives. But I felt that being open about aspects of work in which we could improve demonstrated our straightforwardness. Plus, it showed that listening was one of our values. This technique also allowed new employees to meet people.

Impact

Our new starts integrated quickly, and we had an amazing culture with incredible engagement and buzz. Though the method worked, it didn't last unfortunately, due to external pressures and a new management structure with a command- and control-culture.

Authors' Comments: From Good Practice to Inclusion Nudge

We like this good practice, and see that a **"FEEL THE NEED" Inclusion Nudge** could be designed to leverage the full potential of this practice and sustain support for this and the culture.

For example, start collecting the feedback that the new hires have gathered from employees on the organisational culture. Essentially, culture is *"how things get done around here"* and is reflective of the *underlying beliefs* and *assumptions* of the organisation. For leaders it can be hard to know what an employees' experience with the organisational culture is like. Either they are so accustomed to it that it is invisible or the flow of information on employees' experience is inadequate.

Collecting the findings of the new employees' interviews (who are looking with fresh eyes) and sharing them with senior leaders can help spotlight any issues on inclusion. Display real-life quotes (first-person) in speech bubbles on the wall of the management conference room and instruct them to walk around to read them. Ask them to give some suggestion on how the employees experience the culture/workplace and write this up. Then visually display any common patterns you have pulled from the data and have the managers identify gaps between reality and their perception/assumptions.

NOTE: We have since heard that Flora has implemented other steps with this good practice that are coming close to being an Inclusion Nudge. We have decided to keep this example here in its original submitted form for learning purposes, as it illustrates the intersection of a really good practice and Inclusion Nudges.

Good Practice:

RETENTION OF SENIOR EMPLOYEES (AGE 55+)

Submitted by: Karin Middelburg van Goinga, company anonymous

Why

In one company, people over 55 were asking to retire early due to high stress levels. They also felt demotivated because their work experience was not valued. The company wanted to offer different types of employment to people in different lifecycle stages as part of I&D.

The Good Practice

Once a year, HR sends managers a list of employees who are turning 55, along with a checklist of topics to include as part of the *"seniority conversations"*.

How

First, we gathered all employees over 55 and had an open discussion on their issues and wishes. HR then set up a small working group that came up with suggestions for how to tackle the issues raised. Proposals to management were as follows:

- Managers should ask employees over 55 if they would like to include a *"seniority conversation"* as part of a regular performance review.
- These employees would be offered the opportunity to mentor younger employees, if they were interested.
- They could work part-time, with a maximum reduction of 20%, while keeping their company pension contribution at the same level.

Once these suggestions were approved, all managers were informed. The resulting discussions became an avenue for the manager to express the senior employee's value, as well as a chance to discuss any career development goals (to counter the bias that mature employees may not want career development). With the trend toward rising pension ages and longer working years, a 55-year-old employee may have another 10-15 years in the workplace.

Impact

Employees felt it was easier to discuss questions related to work-life balance and appreciated the opportunity to work less while keeping their pension levels. Some employees were surprised, as they did not consider they had any age-related issues. Therefore, the voluntary nature of the seniority talk was important: it took place only if the employee agreed. The company retained the experience of the older employees, and several of them worked reduced hours until retirement.

Authors' Comments: From Good Practice to Inclusion Nudge

An Inclusion Nudge could be designed within this Good Practice to challenge the implicit association that older employees do not want learning and development support or career discussions. For example:

"FEEL THE NEED" Inclusion Nudge:

"Aha moments" could be used to challenge implicit associations. For example pull data from your internal employee survey. Show managers similarities between employees under 55 and above 55 on i.e. career motivation, stress, part time wishes etc.

"PROCESS" Inclusion Nudge:

Could be designed to ensure that all employees, regardless of age, are enrolled automatically as a default in career development courses. It is not mandatory, but merely an opt out version instead of an opt-in opportunity.

"FRAMING" Inclusion Nudge:

Make flex work the default for all employees, regardless of age.

Good Practice:

SURFACING UNSPOKEN MYTHS ABOUT INCLUSION & DIVERSITY

Submitted by: Anita Curle, Global D&I Learning Portfolio Manager, Shell Canada, Ltd.

Why

To help leaders understand the difference between what "Inclusion" is and is not, and to spur further dialogue on the topic of inclusion.

The Good Practice

A provocative statement about inclusion is shared with participants. Participants then must show if they either "agree" or "disagree" by holding up a paddle that has either "agree" on one side or "disagree" on the other. Participants must choose an answer. The facilitator leads a short dialogue/discussion after each question.

How

Decide first on how much time you have and allow about 5 minutes per question. Design the questions to invoke debate on the topic of Inclusion. Start with a fun and easy question such as "Inclusion means giving everybody hugs". Some real sample questions could be:

Inclusion is about involving everyone in decision making.

My team members are authentic at work.

After each question facilitate a debate and dialogue. The best questions are ones where there is a mix of agreement and disagreement from the participants. The idea is to further engage your audience and participants on the topic of Inclusion so they can understand different perspective on the topic and have a better sense of what Inclusion is and is not.

Paddles can be made up through a local printer, or if cost is an issue you can simply create a one page Full Colour document that says "Agree" on one side (suggest you colour green) and then "Red" on the back side (suggest you colour red). People can hold and flip the correct coloured page for their response.

Impact

This exercise is particularly impactful following the "Reader's Theatre" exercise. It is an excellent way to get Leader's hearts and minds into the topic of inclusion. This exercise is excellent for setting context prior to doing skill building inclusion activities. This exercise was recently completed as part of the Pilot for a new course "Performance through Inclusion" for Senior Leaders at Shell on the topic of Inclusion. The hand held paddles made the game very interactive and engaging (the participants wanted to keep the paddles for their teams).

This idea was originally introduced to Anita by Mind Gym. It is simple and effective and was quite powerful to engage an audience on the topic of inclusion.

Authors' Comments

This is an excellent exercise working with the rational, reflective mind which can follow up on the "FEEL THE NEED" Inclusion Nudge of the "Reader's Theatre" or any other "eye opener" Inclusion Nudge. As we talked about in the introduction of this Guidebook, a full range of good techniques and approaches are needed to help make progress on inclusion and diversity. Inclusion Nudges are one of these, however not the only approach. By combining various techniques, I&D practitioners will be well equipped to help drive sustainable behavioural and culture change. In this case, if first a "FEEL THE NEED" Inclusion Nudge is used which catches the participant by surprise and sheds light on the contradiction of their automatic thinking and actions with their professed goals, then offering as a follow up an exercised like this one that Anita uses could lead to greater open-mindedness and self-awareness of the participants as the exercises pushes further along on reflecting about inclusion and diversity in the organisation. Working hand-in-hand, the Inclusion Nudge and the Exercise help to position sustainable change for greater inclusion.

It is also possible to re-work some good practices to have Inclusion Nudges within them. Remember that Inclusion Nudges work on the subconscious, automatic mind and with a "FEEL THE NEED" Inclusion Nudge, it is aimed at addressing motivation to align behaviour to intentions. A "FEEL THE NEED" Inclusion Nudge would offer up an 'a-ha' or 'eye opener' where the individual realises the contradiction between their unreflected beliefs and automatic actions with what they what to actually be doing.

I&D Good Practice vs Inclusion Nudge

SECTION SUMMARY

Keep in mind that our suggestions on these Inclusion Nudges are not some we have tested. These are what we suggest based on our insight in behavioural economics. This is what we would try out to leverage more of the potential in the good practices.

We hope that through greater understanding of behavioural economics and the Inclusion Nudge concept, and with your experimentation with the design of Inclusion Nudges in your organisations, future editions of this Guidebook will contain more examples of impactful Inclusion Nudges.

Thank you again to all who submitted content for this Guidebook. If your contribution does not appear, it was an example of a good practice. Since it was not our intention to publish a Guidebook of good practices, we have included only the ones that show how Inclusion Nudges could be designed within a good practice. Keep looking for where you can design nudges for inclusion, and please share these with the Global Inclusion Nudges Community via the book's website www.inclusion-nudges.org. If you would like some assistance, we are also available to work with you and/or organisations to guide through the process of designing nudges.

Authors' Final Comments

Become an Expert as You Practice and Keep Sharing

Over the past years, we have facilitated workshops, one-on-one coaching sessions and learning labs on the concept of Inclusion Nudges with leaders, concept owners, change agents, and I&D colleagues in many countries and sectors. The effort has resonated strongly, and we are pleased to see so many applying this concept. We strongly believe this approach will help take insights about the unconscious mind to a practical application level in our efforts to develop more inclusive organisations. We also believe that with this approach we can join forces and create a paradigm shift in the field of Inclusion & Diversity. In 2015, we were named 'Top 10 Diversity Consultants' in the Global Diversity List, which is supported by *The Economist* for this innovative work on Inclusion Nudges and global sharing initiative.

Getting buy-in for I&D seems to be a major issue for many internal practitioners. We see an overweight of "FEEL THE NEED" Inclusion Nudges in the contributions. As internal change agents, we will more easily get buy-in from leaders and promote behavioural shifts that keep up with changes in the global environment without having to convince others about the benefits of inclusiveness. Thus "FEEL THE NEED" Inclusion Nudges are important in paving the way for I&D, but we believe that the "PROCESS" and "FRAMING" Inclusion Nudges have a greater impact in changing the organisational norms that are some of the hidden and most profound barriers to true inclusive and diverse organisations. We encourage our colleagues to work on designing these types of Inclusion Nudges as well.

Our final advice is to practice applying these techniques. Find inspiration in the contributions of peers in this Guidebook, adjust them to fit your organisation, or design new Inclusion Nudges in your organisation. Our personal experiences have been a journey of experiments and learning by doing. We believe that everyone can become a master of nudging for inclusion and we encourage you to share your examples for future versions of this Guidebook, creating a global movement of sharing what works. Visit the website, www.inclusion-iudges.org, for an interactive way to continue your learning and sharing across the Inclusion Nudges Global Community.

If this Guidebook has inspired you to explore further how to design these powerful Inclusion Nudges and involve your internal colleagues, we offer Inclusion Nudges mini-sessions, collaborative assistance and learning labs. We also offer individual Inclusion Nudge coaching on specific challenges in organisations. Details are at the end of this Guidebook.

"Never doubt that a small group of thoughtful, committed citizens can change the world; indeed, it's the only thing that ever has".

– Margaret Mead

dition: 2, January 2016 © T. Nielsen & L. Kepinski, 2016
www.inclusion-nudges.org

References and Additional Resources

BOOKS

BEHAVIOURAL ECONOMICS FOR DUMMIES. Morris Altman, PhD, 2012

BLINDSPOTS: HIDDEN BIASES OF GOOD PEOPLE. Mahzarin R. Banaji and Anthony G. Greenwald, 2013

BLINK: THE POWER OF THINKING WITHOUT THINKING. Malcolm Gladwell, 2006

CHOOSING NOT TO CHOOSE: UNDERSTANDING THE VALUE OF CHOICE. Cass R. Sunstein, 2015.

DESIGNING FOR BEHAVIOR CHANGE: APPLYING PSYCHOLOGY AND BEHAVIOURAL ECONOMICS. Stephen Wendel, 2014

DRIVE: THE SURPRISING TRUTH ABOUT WHAT MOTIVATES US. Daniel Pink, 2009

DRUNK TANK PINK: AND OTHER UNEXPECTED FORCES THAT SHAPE HOW WE THINK FEEL, AND BEHAVE. Adam Alter, 2013

EVERYDAY BIAS: IDENTIFYING AND NAVIGATING UNCONSCIOUS JUDGEMENTS IN OUR EVERYDAY LIVES. Howard Ross, 2014

MADE TO STICK. Chip and Dan Heath, 2007

MISBEHAVING: THE MAKING OF BEHAVIORAL ECONOMICS. Richard H. Thaler, 2015.

MORAL TRIBES: EMOTION, REASON, AND THE GAP BETWEEN US AND THEM. Joshua Greene, 2013

NEUROSCIENCE FOR LEADERSHIP: HARNESSING THE BRAIN GAIN ADVANTAGE. Tara Swart, Kitty Chisolm, and Paul Brown, 2015

NUDGE: IMPROVING DECISIONS ABOUT HEALTH, WEALTH AND HAPPINESS. R.H. Thaler and C.R. Sunstein, 2008

PREDICTABLY IRRATIONAL: THE HIDDEN FORCES THAT SHAPE OUR DECISIONS. Dan Ariely, 2009

REINVENTING DIVERSITY: TRANSFORMING ORGANISATIONAL COMMUNITY TO STRENGTHEN PEOPLE, PURPOSE, AND PERFORMANCE. Howard J. Ross, 2011

SUBLIMINAL: HOW YOUR UNCONSCIOUS MIND RULES YOUR BEHAVIOUR. Leonard Mlodinow, 2012

SWITCH: HOW TO CHANGE THINGS WHEN CHANGE IS HARD. Chip and Dan Heath, 2010

THE DIFFERERENCE. HOW DIVERSITY CREATES BETTER GROUPS, FIRMS, SCHOOLS AND SOCIETIES. Scott E. Page, 2007

THE INCLUSION IMPERATIVE: HOW REAL INCLUSION CREATES BETTER BUSINESS AND BUILDS BETTER SOCIETIES. Stephen Frost, 2014

THE INVENTION OF DIFFERENCE: THE STORY OF GENDER BIAS AT WORK. Binna Kandola, 2013

THE INVISIBLE GORILLA: HOW OUR INTUITIONS DECEIVE US. Christopher Chabris and Daniel Simons, 2009

THE POWER OF HABIT: WHY WE DO WHAT WE DO AND HOW TO CHANGE. Charles Duhigg, 2012

THE SOCIAL ANIMAL. David Brooks, 2011

THE UPSIDE OF IRRATIONALITY: THE UNEXPECTED BENEFITS OF DEFYING LOGIC AT WORK AND AT HOME. Dan Ariely, 2010

THE VALUE OF DIFFERENCE: ELIMINATING BIAS IN ORGANISATIONS. Binna Kandola, 2009

THINKING, FAST AND SLOW. Daniel Kahneman, 2011

THINKING: THE NEW SCIENCE OF DECISION-MAKING, PROBLEM-SOLVING, AND PREDICTION. Edited by John Brockman, 2013

TOP BRAIN, BOTTOM BRAIN: SURPRISING INSIGHTS INTO HOW YOU THINK. Stephen M. Kosslyn, PhD and G. Wayne Miller, 2013

WISER: GETTING BEYOND GROUPTHINK TO MAKE GROUPS SMARTER. Cass R. Sunstein and Reid Hastie, 2015

ARTICLES AND RESEARCH PAPERS

5 WEIGHT LOSS TIPS FROM BEHAVIORAL ECONOMISTS. Carmen Nobel, *Harvard Business Review Working Knowledge,* 13 Feb 2013

AWARENESS REDUCES RACIAL BIAS. Devin G. Pope, Joseph Price, and Justin Wolfers, *ES Working Paper Series,* Economic Studies at Brookings, Feb 2014

BEHAVIORAL ECONOMICS GUIDE. BehavioralEconomics.com, Edited by Alain Samson, 2015

BETTER BY THE BUNCH: EVALUATING JOB CANDIDATES IN GROUPS. Maggie Starvish, *Harvard Business Review Working Knowledge*, 18 June 2012

BLIND AUDITIONS KEY TO HIRING MUSICIANS. Marilyn Marks, *Princeton Weekly Bulletin*, 12 February 2001

HEIDI ROIZEN: CASE STUDY. Kathleen L. McGinn and Nicole Tempest, *Harvard Business School Case Study Collection*, January 2000, revised April 2010

HEIDI ROIZEN: NETWORKING IS MORE THAN COLLECTING LOTS OF NAMES. Joyce Routson, *Insights by Stanford Business*, 1 November 2009

COGNITIVE REPAIRS: HOW ORGANISATIONAL PRACTICES CAN COMPENSATE FOR INDIVIDUAL SHORTCOMINGS. C. Heath, R. Larrick, J. Klayman, *Research in Organisational Behaviour*, vol 20, 1-37, 1998

COLOR-BLINDNESS AND INTERRACIAL INTERACTION. Michael I Norton, Samuel R. Sommers, Evan P. Apfelbaum, Natassia Pura, and Dan Ariely, *Association for Psychological Science*, vol 17, no 11, 2006

EFFECT OF GROUP PRESSURE UPON THE MODIFICATION AND DISTORTION OF JUDGMENT. S.E. Asch, *Groups, Leadership and Men*, Editor H. Guertzkow, Carnegie Press, 1951

EVERYONE STARTS WITH AN A: APPLYING BEHAVIOURAL INSIGHT TO NARROW THE SOCIOECONOMIC ATTAINMENT GAP IN EDUCATION. Nathalie Spencer, *RSA*, 12 March 2014

GENDER EQUALITY: A NUDGE IN THE RIGHT DIRECTION. Iris Bohnet, *Financial Times*, 13 October 2010

GLOBALIZATION AND BUSINESS MASCULINITIES. Connell, Robert W. & Julian Wood, *Men and Masculinities*, vol 7, no 4, 347-364, 2005

HACKING TECH'S DIVERSITY PROBLEM. Joan C Williams, *Harvard Business Review*, October 2014

IS THERE STILL A ROLE FOR JUDGMENT IN DECISION-MAKING? Jim Heskett, *Harvard Business Review Working Knowledge*, 7 Aug 2013

MAKING GREAT DECISIONS. C. Heath & O. Sibony. *McKinsey Quarterly*, April 2013

MAKING STICKK STICK: THE BUSINESS OF BEHAVIORAL ECONOMICS. Leslie John, Michael I. Norton, Michael Norris, *Harvard Business School*, 17 April 2014

MALE CHAMPIONS OF CHANGE LEADERSHIP SHADOW REPORT. *Australian Human Rights Commission*, March 2014

MANGFOLDIGHED GIVER PENGE PÅ BUNDLINJEN (in Danish). Justesen, S., *Survey in ISS*, DK, 2012. Summary: Key findings are that teams composed with max 70% of the same gender, nationality and generation performed 4.9% better than homogenous teams.

MASCULINITIES AND GLOBALISATION. Connell, Robert W., *Men and Masculinities*, vol 1, no 1, 3-23, 1998

NOT FAKING IT: MAKING REAL CHANGE IN RESPONSE TO REGULATION AT TWO SURGICAL TEACHING HOSPITALS. K. Kellogg, *Working Paper, MIT*, 2008

NUDGING: THE CURE FOR CORPORATE GENDER DISCRIMINATION?, *CBS*, 11 August 2011

PRACTITIONERS GUIDE TO NUDGING. *Rotman School of Management, University of Toronto*, March 2013

RSA SOCIAL BRAIN PROJECT. Nathalie Spencer, Jonathan Rowson, Louise Bamfield, *RSA*, March 2014

STEER: MASTERING OUR BEHAVIOUR THROUGH INSTINCT, ENVIRONMENT AND REASON. Matt Grist, *RSA*, June 2010

STUDIES OF INDEPENDENCE AND CONFORMITY: I. A MINORITY OF ONE AGAINST A UNANIMOUS MAJORITY. Asch, S. E., *Psychological Monographs*, vol 70, 1-70, 1956

THE BIAS MAP: BEHAVIOURS FROM INTERGROUP AFFECT AND STEREOTYPES. Cuddy, Fiske, & Glick, *Journal of Personality & Social Psychology*, vol 92, no 4, 631-648, 2007

THE BUSINESS OF BEHAVIORAL ECONOMICS. Leslie John and Michael Norton, *Harvard Business Review Working Knowledge Newsletter,* 11 Aug 2014

THE CASE AGAINST RACIAL COLOR-BLINDNESS. Carmen Nobel, *Harvard Business Review Working Knowledge,* 13 Feb 2012

THE HEIGHT LEADERSHIP ADVANTAGE IN MEN AND WOMEN: TESTING EVOLUTIONARY PSYCHOLOGY PREDICTIONS ABOUT THE PERCEPTIONS OF TALL LEADERS. N.M. Blacker et al. *Group Processes Intergroup Relations*, vol 16, no 1, 17-27, January 2013

WHEN PERFORMANCE TRUMPS GENDER BIAS: JOINT VERSUS SEPARATE EVALUATIONS. Working Paper. Bohnet, A. van Geen, M.H. Bazerman, *Harvard Business School*, March 2012

WHY DON'T WE BELIEVE NON-NATIVE SPEAKERS? THE INFLUENCE OF ACCENT ON CREDIBILITY. S. Lev-Ari and B. Kaysar, *Journal of Experimental Social Psychology*, vol 46, no 3, 2010

WHY YOUR BRAIN LOVES GOOD STORYTELLING. Paul J. Zak, *Harvard Business Review Blog*, 28 October 2014

WOMEN MATTER, *McKinsey & Co*, Annual Reports from 2002-2015

OTHER SOURCES

10 QUESTIONS FOR NOBEL LAUREATE DANIEL KAHNEMAN, Time, You Tube, 26 November 2011

ALEX LASKEY: HOW BEHAVIORAL SCIENCE CAN LOWER YOUR ENERGY BILL, TED Talk, February 2013

DAN ARIELY: WHAT IS BEHAVIORAL ECONOMICS?, You Tube, June 2011

DESIGN TO NUDGE AND CHANGE BEHAVIOUR: SILLE KRUKOW, TEDxCopenhagen, 4 October 2013

DRIVE: THE SURPRISING TRUTH ABOUT WHAT MOTIVATES US, RSA Animation
Facilitated by Daniel Pink, You Tube, 1 April 2010

GENDER GAPS IN THE WORKPLACE (GENDER EQUALITY NUDGES), Iris Bohnet,
12 July 2011

**HOW YOUR UNCONSCIOUS MIND RULES YOUR BEHAVIOUR: LEONARD
MLODINOW**, TEDxReset, 25 April 2013

IT'S THE SITUATION, NOT THE PERSON, DAN HEATH, FAST COMPANY, You Tube,
16 September 2010

MAKING STRATEGY SIMPLE, DAN HEATH, FAST COMPANY, YOU TUBE, 16
September 2010

NUDGE THEORY, Wikipedia

NUDGE, THE ANIMATION: HELPING PEOPLE MAKE BETTER CHOICES. The
Rotman School, 12 June 2013

NUDGE: AN OVERVIEW, RICHARD THALER, You Tube, July 29, 2011

PREDICTABLY IRRATIONAL - BASIC HUMAN MOTIVATIONS, Dan Ariely,
TEDxMidwest, You Tube, 29 August 2012

**SWITCH: SHRINK THE CHANGE WITH ONE-MINUTE PRAISINGS, DAN HEATH,
FAST COMPANY**, You Tube, 2 September 2010

THE MARVELS AND THE FLAWS OF INTUITIVE THINKING, DANIEL KAHNEMAN,
Edge Master Class, 2011

**THE MIGHTY STATISTIC: HOW TO MAKE NUMBERS STICK, DAN HEATH, FAST
COMPANY**, You Tube, 16 September 2010

THE PERSUASION OF SAYING YES, DR. ROBERT CIALDINI, You Tube, 26
November 2012

THE PUZZLE OF MOTIVATION, TED Talk, Daniel Pink, 25 August 2009

THE SOCIAL ANIMAL, DAVID BROOKS, RSA Conference 2012 Keynote, 29
February 2012

THE THEORY OF FUN NUDGES (thetheoryoffun.com) to think out of the box,
using fun to change behaviour

WANT TO MOTIVATE PEOPLE? GET THEM OUT OF MASLOW'S BASEMENT, DAN HEATH, FAST COMPANY, You Tube, 16 September 2010

WANT YOUR ORGANISATION TO CHANGE? PUT FEELINGS FIRST, DAN HEATH, FAST COMPANY, You Tube, 16 September 2010

WHY CHANGE IS SO HARD, DAN HEATH, FAST COMPANY, You Tube, 16 September 2010

THE AUTHORS' WORK ON INCLUSION NUDGES FEATURED IN:

- **THE UNITED NATIONS WOMEN EMPOWERMENT PRINCIPLES (WEP) GLOBAL CONFERENCE,** Presentation, New York, March 2012
- **THE UNITED NATIONS WOMEN EMPOWERMENT PRINCIPLES (WEP) GLOBAL CONFERENCE,** Presentation, Geneva, June 2013
- **THE GLOBAL WOMEN INTERNATIONAL NETWORKING (WIN) CONFERENCE,** Workshop, Prague, October 2013
- **THE COUNCIL FOR DIVERSITY IN BUSINESS, THE CONFERENCE BOARD,** Presentation, Mannheim September 2013
- **THE US DIVERSITY & INCLUSION EXECUTIVES COUNCIL, THE CONFERENCE BOARD,** Presentation, New York, March 2014
- **THE UNITED NATIONS WOMEN EMPOWERMENT PRINCIPLES (WEP) GLOBAL CONFERENCE,** Presentation, New York, March 2014
- **THE GUARDIAN,** Reference in live blog from the United Nations WEP, March 2014
- **THE HUFFINGTON POST,** Reference in Article by Nia Joynson-Romanzina, 2014
- **LEDELSE I DAG,** Danish Leadership Journal, Article, 2014
- **GERMAN DIVERSITY CHARTER DOSSIER,** Article, 2014
- **UNITED NATIONS WEP,** Global Webcast, May 2014

- **THE FUTURE OF WORK, HOT SPOTS MOVEMENT**, Case Study, Global Article, May 2014
- **CITY OF COPENHAGEN CONFERENCE**, Conference Presentation, Copenhagen, February 2014
- **THE FUTURE EMPLOYEES**, Conference Presentation, Copenhagen, June 2014
- **THE CONFERENCE BOARD: THE FUTURE OF DIVERSITY & INCLUSION**, Global Webcast, May 2014
- **THE CONFERENCE BOARD'S THE EVOLUTION OF D&I MANAGEMENT**, Global Article, Fall 2014
- **HR CRANET CONFERENCE**, Workshop, Copenhagen, September 2014
- **THE FUTURE OF WORK, LONDON BUSINESS SCHOOL**, Global Webcast, September 2014
- **CITY OF COPENHAGEN, DIVERSITY CHARTER MEMBER COMPANIES**, Workshops, Copenhagen, September-October 2014
- **THE GLOBAL WOMEN INTERNATIONAL NETWORKING (WIN) CONFERENCE**, Workshop, Berlin, October 2014
- **IBM BUSINESS CONNECT CONFERENCE FOR THE PUBLIC SECTOR**, Workshop, Copenhagen, October 2014
- **THE UNITED NATIONS, GLOBAL COMPACT & UN WOMEN WEP "CALL TO ACTION ON UNCONSCIOUS BIAS"**, Global Article, Fall 2014
- **STRATEGY DAYS LEARNING CONFERENCE**, Keynote Presentation, Germany, October 2015
- **THE CONFERENCE BOARD**, Global Webcast, February 2015
- **ICON GLOBAL DIVERSITY & INCLUSION CONFERENCE**, Barcelona, February 2015
- **THE CONFERENCE BOARD, HUMAN CAPITAL WATCH™: "THE EVOLUTION OF D&I MANAGEMENT"**, Global Webcast, February 2015
- **AARHUS BUSINESS CLUB**, Keynote Presentation, Aarhus, April 2015
- **DIVERSITY CHARTER AARHUS MUNICIPALITY**, Keynote Presentation, Aarhus, April 2015

- **CSR CONFERENCE RATKAISUN PAIKKA, FIBS**, Presentation, Helsinki, May 2015
- **EXECUTIVE NETWORK DENMARK**, Leadership Masterclass, Copenhagen, May 2015
- **HR VISION CONFERENCE**, Keynote Presentation, Amsterdam, June 2015
- **EUROPEAN WOMEN'S MANAGEMENT DEVELOPMENT (EWMD),** Global webcast, October 2015
- **LEDERNE CONFERENCE**, Keynote Presentation, Copenhagen, October and November 2015
- **ANNUAL HR MINDS FORUM**, Keynote Presentation, Vienna, March 2016
- **UN WEP ANNUAL GLOBAL CONFERENCE**, Workshop, New York, March 2016
- **FORUM FOR WORKPLACE INCLUSION GLOBAL CONFERENCE**, Workshop, Minneapolis, March 2016
- **OPEN UNIVERSITY DENMARK**, Lectures, Copenhagen, April 2016
- **SOCIAL INNOVATION PROGRAM, AMANI INSTITUTE KENYA AND BRAZIL,** Presentation, April & September 2016

Additionally, Lisa and Tinna have facilitated interactive sessions and Learning Labs in many private, public and non-profit organisations across a wide range of sectors on the challenges of the unconscious mind and techniques of Inclusion Nudges.

About the Authors and Contact Information

Lisa Kepinski
Inclusion Institute
lisa.kepinski@inclusion-institute.com

Lisa has more than 20 years of Inclusion & Diversity (I&D) experience as a senior executive with AXA, Microsoft and Hewlett-Packard. She is the founder and CEO of the **INCLUSION INSTITUTE,** focused on D&I research, consultancy, training and coaching. Her special expertise in organisational development integrated with I&D make her a unique resource for change at all levels, from the individual to the systems level. Lisa integrates new approaches from areas outside of I&D, and works with organisations to set strategy, apply innovative approaches, and deliver upon pragmatic actions to achieve results.

Lisa has been on the advisory boards of Catalyst Europe and W.I.N., she was a founding member of a European-based Global D&I Network, and for two years a faculty member of the Conference Board's "D&I Academy" teaching new I&D leaders. Additionally, Lisa coaches new I&D practitioners. She co-teaches a course on OD Skills for Change Agents. She is a frequent speaker on I&D topics such as Inclusion Nudges, Bias, Gender Inclusion, and I&D Strategy.

Lisa has a Bachelor's degree in Social Psychology and a Master's in Linguistics, with a specialization on gender communications. She has lived in five countries and travelled extensively. Born and educated in the U.S., Lisa has worked in Europe for more than 15 years. She lives permanently in Germany with her husband and their two daughters who are all originally from Poland.

Tinna C. Nielsen
Move the Elephant for Inclusiveness
tinna@movetheelephant.org

Tinna is an anthropologist and behavioural economist by heart and profession. Since 2010 she has worked as Head of Diversity, Inclusion and Collaboration (2010-15) for Arla Foods, one of the world's largest dairy cooperatives. Previous to this, she worked for the Danish Institute for Human Rights. For the past 14 years, her passion has been to promote behavioural, cultural and systemic changes for inclusiveness. For this purpose she founded the socio-economic organisation MOVE THE ELEPHANT FOR INCLUSIVENESS in 2013.

She has extensive experience in leadership development at all levels and in all functions, design and facilitation of interactive training, and experimental learning, along with team, cultural and organisational development focusing on innovation, performance and change. In every aspect of organisational and people development, Tinna focuses on mitigating unconscious bias and designing Inclusion Nudges.

Tinna has been honoured by the World Economic Forum as Young Global Leader 2015. She will be an active member of the YGL community for 6 years contributing to solutions that improve the state of the World. She is also a fellow at the RSA, Royal Society of Arts, a former member of the executive committee of Diversity in Business Council and a faculty member of the "D&I Academy" at The Conference Board. She is a keynote speaker and workshop facilitator in many different domains such as the United Nations, The International Committee of the Red Cross, public schools and private and public organisations. She lives in Denmark with her family of five and has lived in France and the U.S.

nclusion Nudges Learning Process

Helping Our Brains Make Better Decisions for Inclusive Organisations

In addition to this Guidebook, Lisa and Tinna work with organizations on Inclusion Nudges. We offer an engaging, full learning process designed to help organisations move beyond awareness of unconscious bias. Awareness alone does not lead to cultural and behavioural change. To make it stick, a combined approach is needed on understanding, feeling, motivation, behaviours, and organisational processes. We have designed an effective learning process and tools to support individuals in designing Inclusion Nudges. Our focus is to share our knowledge and expertise with organisations so they can learn how to carry this practice forward internally and with hopes for them to become a contributing part of the Global Inclusion Nudges Community inspiring other by sharing their own Inclusion Nudges.

To Start: INCLUSION NUDGES Inspiration/Introduction Session (3 hr session)

:: The Human Mind

:: Behavioural Drivers

:: Behavioural Economics

:: Inclusion Nudges

:: Practical Application to Specific Organisational Challenges

:: Introducing Audit & Design Process

To Design: INCLUSION NUDGES Full Learning Process

(See Illustration on the next page)

INCLUSION NUDGES

Practical Techniques for Behaviour, Culture, & System Change to Mitigate Unconscious Bias & Create Inclusive Organisations

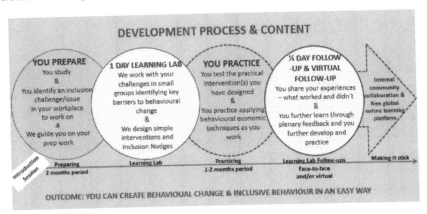

Who should attend?

Key decision makers and processes owners. Examples: D&I practitioners, HR BPs, managers of HR functions, business leaders, marketing, communications, CSR, research & innovation, safety, well-being, and anyone working with behavioural change in organisations.

Contact us to schedule for your organization:

Lisa Kepinski
Inclusion Institute
lisa.kepinski@inclusion-institute.com

Tinna C. Nielsen
Move the Elephant for Inclusiveness
tinna@movetheelephant.org

Endnotes

---

[1] Eric Dziedzic, CEO, CRxSolutions

[2] In this document, we use the term "Inclusion & Diversity" (I&D) instead of the traditional "Diversity & Inclusion" (D&I). In our experience, an approach that begins with inclusion produces an environment that is more receptive to a positive stance on the value of diversity. We do not mean to diminish the work on diversity, but rather to offer an alternative starting point for organisations.

[3] The **GLOBAL DIVERSITY & INCLUSION BENCHMARKS (GDIB)**, by Julie O'Mara and Alan Richter, is available free of charge through the Diversity Collegium. Go to: http://diversitycollegium.org/downloadgdib.php

[4] To review the Creative Commons license, go to: http://creativecommons.org/licenses/by-nc-sa/4.0/

[5] It is sometimes brought up in I&D discussions that "gender" (usually meaning "women") is *not* part of I&D work. Sometimes the work is called "Diversity and Gender" or "Equity and Gender" or some variant of this. This is rooted in a view of the overall sheer numbers of women does not warrant the label of "minority", and a belief that I&D work is only focused on the "minority". The authors' perspective is that I&D is *not* a minority focus, but inclusive of all employees.

[6] See References Section for these book citation details

[7] Paul J. Zak. **"WHY YOUR BRAIN LOVES GOOD STORYTELLING"**, *Harvard Business Review Blog*, 28 October 2014

[8] N.M. Blacker et al. **"THE HEIGHT LEADERSHIP ADVANTAGE IN MEN AND WOMEN: TESTING EVOLUTIONARY PSYCHOLOGY PREDICTIONS ABOUT THE PERCEPTIONS OF TALL LEADERS"**. Group Processes Intergroup Relations, vol 16, no 1, 17-27, January 2013

[9] Condry, John and Condry, Sandra. **"SEX DIFFERENCES: A STUDY IN THE EYE OF THE BEHOLDER,"** *Child Development*, vol 47, 812–819, 1976

[10] Source: Professor Frank Flynn, Stanford Graduate Business School http://www.gsb.stanford.edu/news/headlines/wim_martin07.shtml

[11] **"WHY DON'T WE BELIEVE NON-NATIVE SPEAKERS? THE INFLUENCE OF ACCENT ON CREDIBILITY"**. S. Lev-Ari & B. Kaysar, 2010

[12] **NUDGE**, Thaler & Sunstein, p6

[13] Photo sourced from
http://www.bing.com/images/search?q=fly%20in%20urinals&FORM=BILH1#view=detail
&id=295FBC62FFD87B96D7B82B89FC285F8A87BD2333&selectedIndex=33

[14] Photo sourced from
https://loosingthefatgirl.files.wordpress.com/2013/10/plates.png

[15] From authors' discussions with Elaine Yarbrough referencing Barbara Bunker
and Billie Alban

[16] Photo sourced from: http://imgur.com/gallery/6EgAe

[17] Kurtz & Saks, 1996

[18] Notably by Iris Bohnet, Harvard Kennedy School. See Reference Section.

[19] Dan Heath, Richard Thaler, Future of Work LBS (Lynda Gratton and team),
Elisabeth Kelan, The Conference Board, The United Nations Women
Empowerment Principles (WEP), and more

[20] **"STEER: MASTERING OUR BEHAVIOUR THROUGH INSTINCT, ENVIRONMENT
AND REASON"**, RSA Social Brain Project. See Reference Section

[21] Inspiration: Case study experiment, **"HEIDI VS. HOWARD"**
www.europeanbusinessreview.com/?p=6785 See Reference Section.

[22] Cook Ross, http://cookross.com/

[23] Project Implicit: https://implicit.harvard.edu/implicit/takeatest.html

[24] Source of inspiration: Research by Cuddy, Fiske, & Glick. See Reference
Section.

[25] See:
C:\Users\TOT\Downloads\http:\www.hbs.edu\faculty\Pages\profile.aspx?facId=491042
&facInfo=pub

[26] Contributor prefers to be listed as anonymous. For more information about
this and any other anonymous submissions, please contact the authors.

[27] Casciaro & Lobos, 2005

[28] See: https://www.humanrights.gov.au/sites/default/files/document/publication/
MCC-LeadershipShadow_210314.pdf See Reference Section

[29] See: http://www.washingtonpost.com/blogs/wonkblog/wp/2014/02/25/what-the-
nba-can-teach-us-about-eliminating-racial-bias/

[30] Source of inspiration: **WOMEN MATTER 2**, McKinsey & Co, 2008. See
Reference Section for McKinsey Women Matters series

[31] A good reference on flex work/agile work is **FUTURE WORK: CHANGING
ORGANISATIONAL CULTURE FOR THE NEW WORLD OF WORK**. Alison Maitland
& Peter Thomson, 2014

[32] A good source of inspiration is the **TIMEWISE POWER PART TIME LIST**: http://timewisefoundation.org.uk/our-work/power-part-time/2013-winners

[33] Source of inspiration: **MUSICIAN AUDITIONING PROCESS IN SYMPHONY ORCHESTRAS, BLIND AUDITIONS KEY TO HIRING MUSICIANS.** Marilyn Marks, *Princeton Weekly Bulletin*, 12 February 2001

[34] Found on YouTube at https://www.youtube.com/watch?v=ubNF9QNEQLA

[35] Justesen, 2011, p. 2007

[36] Justesen, 2011

[37] Gratton et.al 2007

[38] **THE 70% HOMOGENEITY QUICK TEST** is available via Innoversity Academy at www.innoversity.dk

[39] See innoversity.org for more research results

[40] Justesen, 2011

[41] blog.hbr.org: **ARE WOMEN BETTER LEADERS THAN MEN?,** J. Zenger and J. Folkman, 15 March 2012

[42] See **DRIVE**, Daniel Pink, to learn more about "intrinsic motivation". See Reference Section

[43] Found on YouTube at: http://www.youtube.com/watch?v=cFdCzN7RYbw

[44] **SWITCH: WHEN CHANGE IS HARD,** Dan & Chip Heath, 2010 and the Social Brain Project. See Reference Section

[45] See "List of Cognitive Biases" on Wikipedia

[46] David Perkins, a geneticist, coined the term "myside bias" referring to a preference for "my" side of an issue. Baron, p.195, 2000

[47] **STATUS QUO BIAS IN DECISION MAKING.** W. Samuelson and R. Zeckhauser, *Journal of Risk and Uncertainty* vol 1, 7–59, 1988

[48] **ANOMALIES: THE ENDOWMENT EFFECT, LOSS AVERSION, AND STATUS QUO BIAS**. D. Kahneman, J.L. Knetsch, and R.H. Thaler, *Journal of Economic Perspectives,* vol 5, no 1, 193–206, 1991

[49] **SOCIAL IDENTITY AND INTERGROUP BEHAVIOR.** H. Tajfel, 1974

[50] http://www.yale.edu/infantlab/Our_Studies.html

[51] **STUDIES OF INDEPENDENCE AND CONFORMITY: I. A MINORITY OF ONE AGAINST A UNANIMOUS MAJORITY**. S.E. Asch, *Psychological Monographs*, vol 70, 1-70, 1956

[52] **MASCULINITIES AND GLOBALISATION.** Robert W. Connell, *Men and Masculinities* vol 1, no 1, 3-23, 1998 & **GLOBALIZATION AND BUSINESS MASCULINITIES.** Connell, Robert W. and Wood, Julian, *Men and Masculinities* vol 7, no 4, 347-364, 2005

83797560R00146

Made in the USA
Middletown, DE
15 August 2018